FRUGALITY FOR DEPRESSIVES:

Money-saving tips for those who find life a little harder

By Abigail Perry

To my mom, for all the helpful information and tireless, good-humored editing. And to Tim for his love and support – and for patiently allowing me even more time in front of a computer.

Table of Contents

Foreword

I've been blogging for nearly eight years about imperfect money management. One of my first posts was about how I was "not the Martha Stewart of frugality."

Of course, the idea that anyone is perfectly frugal is laughable. Everyone makes mistakes. Everyone has limits – not that you'd know that by looking online.

Thanks to the Internet, there's no end to examples of *everyone doing it better than we are*. Everyone else excels, has it together and otherwise annoys us with apparent perfection. Pinterest alone could keep even healthy people in a permanent state of guilty misery.

So what happens when you're not healthy? Envy, dejection, even more guilty misery, and far too many pins about cheap and natural cleaning agents.

To be clear, "healthy" doesn't just mean chronic health problems or disabilities. People with those issues do often have extra limitations, but that's overlooking a very obvious population: depressives.

Depression *is* a health problem. Yet too many people think of it as something to get over or something that goes away for good with the proper medication.

It's true that some depression is situational: a *very* bad relationship, a toxic work environment, the loss of a loved one. However, many people are depressives for life. Medication and therapy can lessen symptoms but they won't eradicate the problem.

I was diagnosed as a depressive at age 21. Almost a decade – and quite a lot of frustration and mental anguish – later, someone finally realized that it was bipolar depression, rather than the unipolar version most depressives have.

My type (bipolar II) tends to exhibit far tamer mania than classic bipolar disorder. In that, I'm lucky. But the deep despair remains, often even amid manic episodes.

I'm well-medicated which keeps me, thankfully, non-suicidal and even functional. But that doesn't mean my problems vanish with a pill. I still struggle with things that the mentally healthy find routine, or even simple.

I spent quite a lot of time feeling ashamed of my depression and the limits it creates. I spent perhaps even more time trying to prove that I could power through and do everything "normal" people can.

I'd read wonderful frugal tips but be unable to replicate them. Coupons always created more of a mess than savings – by a long shot. When bad days kept me from leaving the house, I'd miss sales and have to (gasp) pay retail. Food in the fridge frequently went to waste when I couldn't face leftovers, opting instead for fast food or pizza. If that food were in containers, the whole thing would have to be thrown out to avoid my very violent gag reflex. (I have a lot of incomplete Tupperware sets.)

Each failure drove the shame and despair deeper. Each new twist focused my mind on my inability to be the good frugal girl I was raised to be.

That misery made it more difficult to function in other areas of life. This caused more failures, which exacerbated my self-disgust, thereby causing yet more failures. Eventually it would end with me under the covers, hiding from the world. Unfortunately, the world is patiently waiting for you outside the blanket, and sooner or later you'll have to get up to use the bathroom.

At some point – probably while hunkered down in the bed with a trusty stuffed animal – I realized that depression is a real illness.

Yes, yes, I knew *abstractly* it was an illness. I knew I needed medication, which is what you need when you're sick. But it took me years (and a lot of therapy and my husband's pleas) to finally understand that I had a real medical condition.

Even then, it took me a while to truly accept there were things I simply can't do. I can push myself as hard as I like. I can even cajole, exhort or bribe myself, but that doesn't change the fact that I'm sick.

I finally conceded that there are days when I can't manage simple tasks. I could either sit around feeling ashamed of that, or I could work around it.

After this stunning(ly overdue) revelation, I realized that the same held true for my frugal efforts. There will always be things I can't manage. At best, there will be things that I can't manage *that day*.

By constantly refusing to accept that, by trying to always push through, I was personifying the old adage about the definition of insanity. (Feel free to insert your own DSM joke here.) I was doing the same thing over and over, expecting different results.

So I decided to get over it. To get over myself and my ridiculous notion that I should be able to do it all. In fact, I've come to realize that "should" is one of the most dangerous words in the English language. It speaks to expectations – and the expectations we have for ourselves are rarely reasonable, let alone realistic.

So no, I will never be the Martha Stewart of frugality. None of us will; even Martha Stewart is fallible, as her prison record will attest.

What matters is that we find a level of frugality – deeply imperfect though it may be – that is both acceptable and realistic. Failing that, we should at least shoot for realistic.

I'm writing this book in the hopes that these tips and insights – hard-won and, in many cases, hard-lost – will help others find their own equilibrium between saving money and not driving themselves crazy. Or crazier, as the case may be.

So without further ado, here's Frugality for Depressives.

Chapter 1: Forgive yourself

Before we get into the nitty-gritty, I'd like to go a little touchy-feely.

Depression is a disease that tricks us into thinking that we're bad people. We spend quite a bit of our time and energy being our own worst critics. Maybe we even believe that we're a drain on our friends and family.

At any given time I have what I like to call a mental highlight reel, which is more like a lowlight reel. It replays stupid things I've done or said. It even includes things I think *might* have been taken the wrong way.

Many depressives I've talked to experience something similar. Beyond being a danger to our overall mental health, this self-reproach poses another issue: It's incredibly draining.

We depressives start with sub-standard coping abilities and energy. Then we fritter away what little we have on regret and recrimination, leading to what I call the shame spiral.

Generally it starts with a simple, everyday task. Perhaps you have errands that need to get done, but you can't leave the house.

You're annoyed and upset that you can't do something you "should" (there's that word again) be able to do. You tell yourself you're being stupid, ridiculous, or whatever other negative adjective your brain supplies.

The self-criticism makes you feel worse, which deepens your depression. The worse your depression, the lower your coping ability. The lower your coping ability, the fewer things you'll be able to do. The less you're able to do, the more ammunition you have to use against yourself.

When you use that ammo, you feel worse. The worse you feel, the deeper your depression. And so on and so forth until you've spiraled into an abyss of self-loathing and unfinished tasks.

Picture the Swamp of Sadness from *The Neverending Story*. Once you lose hope, you sink into the mud. Sinking into the mud causes you to lose more hope, which makes you sink faster. It's a vicious cycle that ends with the death of a beautiful horse and crying children everywhere. Metaphorically speaking.

You're only human

In the end, you have to forgive yourself in order to stay sane. Or sane-ish, as the case may be.

The people who love you know that you're human. They know that you make mistakes. Yet they're still around. They forgive your flaws, just as you forgive theirs.

In fact, that's the perfect way to look at it: The next time you're berating yourself about a mistake, stop and think how you'd feel if someone you love had made it.

My guess? You'd absolve them in a heartbeat, assuming you thought they needed it at all.

So now you know that you'd be forgiving with someone you love. Next, remember that you're supposed to love yourself. And thanks to the transitive property, you have proof that your "sin" is pardonable.

Getting real

If that still doesn't get through to you, then it's time to look at the hard reality: You can't afford to hate yourself. Not if you want to get anything else done.

For depressives, surviving from day to day takes almost everything we have. Everything is harder, more intimidating and generally more upsetting. What little mental, emotional and physical energy we have must be spent carefully.

It's our most valuable currency, and it's not to be wasted on self-castigation. If you want to do more than just survive – whether you believe you deserve to or not – you need to get over yourself.

Don't get me wrong. I suffered this kind of self-hatred for years. I gave into it. I soaked in it. I let it fill me until I had no hope of ever being a person worthy of love or respect. But eventually I realized that the traditional wailing and gnashing of teeth leads nowhere, other than a dry throat and TMJ.

So I got angry. I was angry that nothing changed. I was angry that my sorrow sucked up time, energy and emotional resources. I got angry about how much I was hurting my husband, Tim, with my ups and downs.

Then I got even angrier when I noticed how much I was blaming myself. Depression was fooling me into being ashamed. It was warping my perceptions until I was mired in my own little world of despair. So I refocused my anger on the disease itself, rather than the symptoms. I was determined to beat it.

And I failed. Spectacularly.

What? Did you think this was going to be a story about triumph? It's not – at least not in the sense most people expect.

A new lens

My triumph wasn't about overcoming depression, magically fixing my brain chemistry and living a "normal" life. It was when my common sense finally overcame the negativity. It was when I realized that there is no room for "should" in a chronically ill person's life, whether the illness is physical, mental or emotional.

After reflection – and therapy! – I decided to throw out any and all expectations of what I *should* be able to do. Then I started scribbling on my newly blank slate.

I took stock of what I could definitely manage:

- My job
- My blog
- Prudent financial decisions (mostly)
- Complete day-to-day errands (eventually)
- Laugh at life (about 80% of the time)

It wasn't much, but it's what I had to work with. Then I set about figuring out how the hell I could make a life, let alone a financially savvy one, around those abilities.

Each time I failed at a frugal venture, I dropped it altogether. For example, Tim's ADD makes using coupons difficult. He avoids it unless I'm with him. That defeated the purpose of my sending him to the grocery store. So we stopped couponing. Since neither of us can cook consistently, we subsisted (expensively) on takeout.

And so on and so forth until I was working with the bare minimum: a job, my blog and trying not to spend unnecessarily (with a broad definition of "unnecessarily").

Next, I started evaluating each aspect of frugality through a new lens. I asked myself whether I *could* do it rather than forcing myself and suffering the fallout. I slowly added things back in: shopping more sales, lowering the food budget, being stricter about general spending, etc.

It turns out that building your life around reality – rather than the fantasy you've constructed – makes things a lot easier. Having realistic expectations means you don't have to forgive yourself as often – and when you do, it's less of a struggle.

Shrug it off

You might wonder why forgiveness is so important. That's simple: You'll need a lot of it.

Most people will experience a fair number of frugal fails. Frugality means changing aspects of your life. Change is often hard, tiring and stressful.

Depressives tend to have less energy and a lower tolerance for stress than the mentally healthy. So change will probably be harder for you. You'll probably have more frugal fails – or the ones you have will be felt more keenly.

If you can't forgive yourself you'll wind up immobilized by frustration, anger and/or hopelessness. And if you're immobilized, you'll have wasted money on this book.

So take a deep breath and prepare yourself for some failure. That preparation will help cushion you when you fall. And remember that you won't be the only one falling. Perfectly healthy people meet the ground more often than you might expect.

Life is a learning curve, and everyone falls off it at some point. You have to think of mistakes as teachable moments, rather than proof that you're worthless. You have to learn to laugh it off or, at the very least, shrug it off. Or just try not to cry… much.

Remember, making a mistake or failing to accomplish something isn't proof that you're a bad person. It just means that you're a person.

Human beings are inherently flawed. So in a way, being imperfect makes you a perfect human.

(Okay, touchy-feeliness is over now. I promise.)

Chapter 2: Imperfect frugality

People tend to treat frugality as an immutable set of rules. If you fail at one, you're out of the club. But if that were the case, there'd be nobody *left* in the club. Or maybe there'd be a few people, but they'd be too annoying to hang out with.

Remember that nothing is absolute. There's no single action you have to take to be considered frugal. No mob of angry frugal villagers will come after you with pitchforks just because you don't reuse Ziploc bags or cut your own hair.

My husband and I both have multiple chronic conditions. As already mentioned, I'm bipolar. I also have chronic fatigue from a near-fatal neurological illness that struck me at 19. My husband, Tim, is a depressive with fibromyalgia and very severe eczema and asthma.

Because of this, some frugal practices just aren't possible for us. As I mentioned, we don't coupon; in fact, we don't even cook. Yet I still consider us to be frugal.

There is no One True Way of frugality. It's a spectrum, and you'll find your spot somewhere on it. That is, as long as you don't give up looking at the first sign of failure. Or the second, third, fourth or… you get the idea.

The sole defining characteristic of frugality is meaningful spending. As my mom likes to say, it's about saving where you can so that you can spend where you want.

The key word here is "can." Everyone practicing frugality will find there are things they can't do – or things that they feel simply aren't worth the savings. You'll have similar experiences, but as a depressive your tolerance will probably be lower.

Still, you don't have to be a frugal maven to see results. Even small savings add up. Any progress is, well, progress. So try one frugal hack at a time. If it works, keep it; if not, move on. You can always come back to it later.

The key to lasting frugality is making sustainable changes. You focus on each aspect until it feels more natural, then you move on to the next challenge. Over time, you'll create a frugal framework that will let you function on a sort of frugal auto-pilot.

Chapter 3: Don't budget

You read that right. I don't think depressives should budget – at least not using the classic model.

I'm referring to one where spending is separated into discrete categories, each with a non-negotiable cap. The budgeter keeps a running tally of expenses throughout the month. He or she will also constantly be on alert for ways to minimize spending.

That's a lot for most depressives to juggle.

Depression affects not just moods, but also memory and concentration. Will you remember to record every expense? When you're out and about, will you be able to remember how much money is left in each category that month? If you can't, how can you know whether that sale on toilet paper is a great deal or a budget buster?

Budgeting can be tough even for healthy people. How could depressives expect it to be feasible?

Our experience

No doubt some depressives *do* manage that kind of budget. Perhaps it even provides some much-needed structure. The rest of us, though, are simply priming ourselves for a slide down the shame spiral.

I myself tried a classic budget for a long time. Alas, our spending was too unpredictable. Having multiple chronic conditions –

including my husband's ADD, with the accompanying impulse spending – meant we were dealt a hand with too many wild cards.

Extra doctor visits or new medications meant more co-pays. Tim sometimes ran out of his inhaler early, and we had to pay $60 out of pocket for a new one. Steroids made him gain weight, causing us to have to buy him a new wardrobe – twice. One health condition or another would flare up, halting any cooking regimen we'd attempted. So it was pizza or fast food (and the accompanying bill) to the rescue.

But the biggest stumbling block by far was finding realistic budget numbers. My depressive brain refused to take reality into account. I budgeted based on what I *wanted* our spending to be, rather than allowing for what I could reasonably expect to happen. (Not that I could ever have reliably predicted the onslaught of financial groin shots we received in a given month.)

Budgeting based on wishful thinking is like shopping for size-2 clothing when you're a size 14. Sure, one day it might fit. Even so, there'll be a long time that you stare at it, hating it for not fitting and hating yourself for not fitting into it. That's energy best spent elsewhere.

But I hadn't figured that out yet. Part of me truly believed that if we just set the numbers, life would fall in line.

I remember setting a $150 food budget for two people who could barely cook and then being devastated, furious and freaked out when we inevitably went over. And don't even get me started on my guesses about medical expenses. (Hint: It was a disaster.)

Perhaps I believed that strict numbers would make us try harder. Instead, they just sent me into mild hysteria every time a new expense reared up.

I was angry at myself, angry at Tim and furious at our illnesses, because they all combined to ruin my perfect budget. Moreover, each time we exceeded the spending cap I felt panicked, hopeless and helpless. It made me less able to cope with the rest of our lives.

So I stopped. Instead I decided to keep tabs on our financial activity and to trim our spending. But I refused to categorize the transactions. Given our unpredictable expenses and my relatively low coping ability, budgeting just didn't make sense.

Obviously not everyone's expenses look like ours. If you're dead set on trying to budget, a classic one may work for you – as long as you can figure out a reasonable amount for each category. (More on this later.)

Budget categories

If you insist on trying to budget, it's important to include as many recurring expenses as possible. Nothing will break a budget faster than forgetting to account for an expenditure.

Let's start with the basics:

- Rent/Mortgage
- Utilities (even if this is a best guess for the first couple of months)
- Groceries/household (some people separate the two)
- Internet
- Cable
- Cell phone
- Gas/transportation
- Entertainment/meals out (again, some people separate the two)
- Retirement contributions (if any)

- Savings
- Stock-up fund (more on this later)
- Any other monthly fees (gym, life insurance, pet insurance, etc.)

These comprise the classic budget. I recommend you start only with those.

Once you're comfortable with the basics of budgeting, consider adding the following categories – preferably no more than two of them a month, to keep things simple.

Emergency fund: Big expenses come along unexpectedly, so you need a cushion. Put a little aside each month, even if it's as small as $10-20. Anything is better than nothing.

Car repair/replacement: If you have an emergency fund, you can choose to do without a car repair fund. Still, you might want to build some savings toward a down payment when your current automobile bites the dust.

Car insurance: Divide your annual premium by 12 (or semi-annual by six), and set that amount aside each month. When the bill comes due, you'll already have the funds.

Pets: Some people prefer to save separate emergency funds for their furry/scaly/feathered friends. At the very least it's good to have a budget category for their food and any annual care.

Holiday gifts: It's smart to save up a little each month in preparation for whichever winter holiday you celebrate. Having a set amount can also help keep you from overspending. All in all, it's a great way to keep the celebration from wrecking your budget.

Hair care: A haircut usually costs $30 or more. Most people visit a salon or barber every four to six weeks, but that may not be reflected in the budget.

Fun money: You need to have at least a little bit of discretionary money, for hobbies, gadgets or other indulgences.

Slush: Shoes and clothes wear out. Friends and relatives selfishly insist on having birthdays and anniversaries *every year*. Kids need to go on field trips or to birthday parties. You can't plan for everything. A slush fund can help.

For any funds you keep in abeyance, I recommend setting up accounts at online banks like Capital One 360. You'll get free checking and better interest rates on savings. Plus you can set up as many savings sub-accounts as you want. It's great for keeping track of various goals. We have 11 of them:

- Emergency fund
- Car
- Car insurance
- Vacation
- Pet
- Washer/dryer fund (we put $2.50 in for each load we do)
- My fun money
- My husband's fun money
- Health insurance
- Taxes (I'm self-employed)
- Saved savings (I'll explain this later in the book)

You certainly don't have to go overboard like us, but I love not having to divert money from one goal to cover another one. It's made things a lot easier.

Before we had dedicated accounts, I never wanted to travel because it meant dipping into savings. After many arguments,

Tim suggested (okay, vehemently insisted) that we start a separate vacation fund.

I'm so glad we did. It's allowed me the peace of mind to stay in a hotel for a birthday or anniversary and even to take short trips to Las Vegas. (Yep, even frugal people can gamble – as long as they budget for it and kiss the money goodbye ahead of time.)

Despite the dizzying number of categories, that's actually the easy part of budgeting. The real challenge is figuring out how much money goes into each one. There are a few ways to do this.

The magic number method

Unfortunately, we sometimes make up our minds before thinking about silly things like rational limits. It could be that your brain has latched onto what feels like the magic number. It seems most common in the grocery category, but it can be true of any area in the budget.

But since magic numbers only exist in your imagination, you need to get real. So increase that amount by 25%. Now you have a figure that might actually work.

Your mind will probably scream in protest. Shush it by reminding yourself that you're not "most" people. You wouldn't expect someone with cancer to stick to an austere budget, would you? Of course not, because illness interferes with your ability to take care of yourself and it can cost you in unexpected ways. Depression is an illness, too. So it's essential to set realistic goals.

The "If they can do it…" method

If you're already reading personal finance blog, you've probably heard various bloggers' budget numbers. You might be tempted to use those to form your own. And it's true that you *can* use those spending caps… sorta.

It's important to model yourself only after people in areas with similar costs of living. If you're in Alaska or Hawaii, don't use the food budget of someone in Phoenix. If you live in LA or New York, you can't base your rent category on rates in a medium Midwestern city.

But let's stick to food, since it's one of the hardest categories to predict. Once you've found someone whose food budget seems reasonable, take that dollar amount and add at least 25%.

I know that increased spending sounds counterintuitive. Once again this comes down to being realistic. Many depressives I know rely on a lot of prepared supermarket dishes, fast food and takeout. Their spending will necessarily be higher than someone who cooks everything from scratch.

Unless you're a foodie or find cooking soothing you probably won't prepare your own meals as often as other people. (And if you *are* a foodie, you'll spend more on ingredients.) It's better to have a slightly plumper budget, which you can reduce over time, than to start too low. Going over budget is stressful, and stress might make you abandon further attempts.

The historical method

The easiest approach is based on your own financial history. Sure, you can measure yourself by some blogger's standards. But you may find it more rewarding to chart your own progress rather than focusing on comparisons to other people.

The first step is to figure out where your finances are right now. You can't improve on an unknown, right? Prepare yourself, though: I guarantee you're not going to like some of what you find. At least a couple of category totals are going to be ugly.

Review the last few months' worth of bank activity. Break your spending into whichever budget categories you've decided on.

Be sure to document this somewhere, and not on a piece of paper that could wind up getting lost. (This is not something you want to have to do all over again.) I prefer Excel because it already has rows and columns and because the AutoSum function makes it easy to list and add up totals.

Once you know what you've been spending, the real work begins: figuring out what you should shoot for.

Finding a realistic number can be very difficult for depressives. Yet if you don't have a realistic goal you're potentially dooming yourself. We depressives can be very hard on ourselves. Having an attainable goal increases your chance of success (and decreases the chance that you'll give up budgeting altogether).

This means setting very generous goals. Your financial progress should be a series of small decreases, even though at times this might feel too slow. Focus on the fact that you *are* making progress. That's what matters.

So no matter how ridiculously large you think your spending is, reduce it by no more than 10% in the first month. Small, sustainable steps are best. Cut too much too fast and you might have to bump the category limits back up. That's disheartening and, again, might even lead to you giving up.

Think I'm overstating things? Let's play out a scenario:

Suppose you currently spend $600 a month on food. I suggest you cut 10% the first month, for a $540 spending cap. Your inclination is probably to be much more ruthless, maybe cutting it as much as 50% for a $300 total food budget. That's still more than most people, right?

But you're asking too much of yourself. Suppose that despite your best efforts you spend around $400 on food. That's a huge decrease; you should be celebrating!

Instead, your self-critical brain will focus on your perceived failure. Conversely, under my 10% guideline you'd be $140 *under* budget.

Repeat the 10% decrease each month until you hit your (actual) magic number. You'll know you're there when you go over budget two months in a row. (Try to consider only months without special circumstances, like out-of-town guests or special holiday meals.)

At that point, increase the spending cap a little to avoid further stress. Then choose a frugal hack to lower your grocery bill (more on that later). If that doesn't work, try another hack – or accept that you've found your spending limit.

Now do the same kind of tracking and reduction for your other budget categories. Remember that you don't have to do them all simultaneously. You can focus on just two or three. If that proves to be too difficult, just work with one category at a time.

What matters is that you concentrate on each area until you're on track toward your goal. Once you're comfortable in each category, you can move on to the next one. Later on in the book, I'll offer some frugal hacks to help you reduce spending in your budget categories.

Tools/software

Once you have concrete numbers it's time to look at some budgeting software. Specifically, the free stuff.

You can absolutely get value out of Quicken and You Need a Budget, but they cost money. You'll get most (if not all) of the same functionality from Mint or Power Wallet, without the drain on your funds. And now that you have spending limits, that's important!

You'll have to link your bank account and credit cards to use these budgeting programs. Then you simply plug in your spending caps for each area. The software automatically allocates each transaction into what it deems the appropriate category.

You'll get an alert as you approach a category limit, which lets you rein in your spending. Sometimes you won't be able to avoid busting the budget, but generally the alert will help you stay in control of your cash.

Budgeting software has helped millions of people keep track of their spending, so I urge you to check it out. That said, I found the programs ultimately more stressful than helpful.

For example, I often found myself re-categorizing certain purchases – or at least parts of them. A toothbrush at the grocery store needed to go under toiletries/household, not the groceries category. A soft drink from the Circle K shouldn't count toward the gas total.

This was a hassle. Worse, I felt panicked by the sheer number of emails warning us that we were reaching – or breaching – our spending limits. Rather than feeling more in control of our money, I felt overwhelmed and powerless.

Mind you, some of this was due to my initial inability to set realistic goals. However, the fact is that the lives of two chronically ill people (and a pet) are full of unexpected expenses. Ultimately, I decided it was no good trying to guess how much we'd spend.

Again, I recommend that you at least try the software for a while. It might be just what you need. But don't feel bad if it doesn't work for you. You can always keep notes yourself: on paper, Excel spreadsheet, dry erase board – whatever works for you.

Assuming, that is, that you want to keep trying the classic budget. There is another way.

Our method: One and done

As I mentioned, I put the kibosh on budgeting about eight years ago – at least, normal budgeting.

Now I simply transfer a set amount into the main checking account once a week. That's all the money we get, and it has to cover food, medical co-pays, household goods, entertainment and any other costs that come our way.

Does this work? Usually. There are times when we have to transfer money after six days or, on a particularly bad week, the fifth day. But by and large we're able to function well within the lump-sum framework.

If funds get gobbled up quickly early in the week, either through carelessness or unexpected expenses, we become more circumspect as the balance lowers. It keeps us honest, but we have money in a secondary checking account as a safety net.

If you try this, it may take time to figure out a suitable weekly amount. I initially chose $250 a week, which quickly proved unworkable. We tried $300, but that was still tough.

It turns out our Goldilocks zone is $350 a week. An average of $50 a day seems to cover most of our expenses, not including utilities and medications/unexpected expenses over $40.

Then again, we have a lot of medical costs. Healthier people may find that they can get by on substantially less. Still, it's better to start a little high and winnow it down over time. Eventually, you'll find the one that – to quote that felonious, fictional little blonde girl – is just right.

Stock-up fund

No matter which method you choose, it's a good idea to have a stock-up fund in your budget. Stocking up is a pillar of frugality: You see a good sale, you take full advantage. But it's even more important for depressives.

During our bad spells it can be impossible to do anything more than get up, go to work, come home and somehow feed ourselves. When trips to the store are out of the question, a stockpile is worth its weight in gold.

But stocking up costs money. If you're stressing about the bottom line you might just stick to your shopping list, no matter how good the sale. A stock-up fund will ease your mind. Having that money lets you buy up every last package of your favorite cereal without ruining the monthly budget.

Chapter 4: The latte factor

Anyone who knows anything about frugality either groaned or sighed upon seeing this chapter. That's because most of us are sick unto death of hearing about the latte factor, i.e., the idea that if you just skipped *one coffee a day* you'll retire rich! (Okay, that may be oversimplifying it.)

While I'm just as tired of this ubiquitous point as everyone else, it's an important one for those of you just getting into frugality. So I'm making this sacrifice for you. (You're welcome.)

The latte factor is simply the idea that small things add up.

- That $4 latte you get on the way to work? That's more than $80 each month – or $960 a year.
- Buying lunch every work day is easily $35 a week, which is $140 a month or $1,680 a year. And that's if you're only buying value meals!
- Those semi-monthly manicures are $480 to $720 a year.
- An after-work beer even three times a week adds up to about $500 a year.

Few of us think $1 to $3 here and there is a big deal. At least, not until we do the math. Then we think about it *a lot.*

The good thing about a budget – whatever form yours takes – is that it makes you more aware of your spending. When you do that, you'll start to notice the cumulative effect of these small purchases. Chances are that'll be enough to bring you up short.

Then it's just a matter of not going overboard. You don't have to cut out *all* lattes. Buy one or two a week, and make coffee at home the rest of the time. Making the lattes less commonplace will make them feel more like a treat, which means you get more value from your spending.

Have lunch out *once* a week. The rest of the time, pack your lunch the night before and stick it in the fridge. Then you can just grab it and go in the morning. Again, you'll get a lot more satisfaction from that weekly meal out than you would from daily burgers and fries.

If beautifully polished nails matter (and you can't just do your own) try waiting a full month between manicures. Heck, even switching to every third week will save at least $140 over the course of a year.

Cut down to one night a week at the bar. Or just have people over to your place for a drink. The alcohol is cheaper and you get to choose what's on TV!

The nice thing about the latte factor is that it works in both directions: Just as little expenses add up quickly, so too do little savings.

One way to remind yourself of that is to create a saved savings budget category. Each time you save $1 with a coupon, throw that much into the account. Put in $4 each day that you choose drip coffee made at home. You'll be surprised how much accumulates by the end of the month – and it will motivate you to keep up the good work. (More on this subject later.)

Chapter 5: Nix the coupons (mostly)

Disorder upsets even healthy people. It can be worse for depressives. Granted, this doesn't stop me from living in a cluttered mess. But I find it very upsetting!

My experience

I started couponing when we moved to Phoenix. Local stores round coupons up to $1. How's a frugal gal to resist?

So I gave it my all. I even bought a little binder and filled it with the plastic sheets that hold collectible cards. I kept the coupons organized by section: toiletries, cleaning supplies, desserts, etc. Bless my little over-optimistic heart.

I subscribed to the Sunday paper and diligently cut out the offers and discounts, slotting them into the sleeves. I was determined and on the ball… right up until I wasn't.

One week I wasn't up for dealing with the paper on Sunday and put it off. By Wednesday, it was pretty clear that I wasn't going to get around to it, yet I kept the paper on the coffee table. The next Sunday brought a second paper that I didn't touch, which started the guilt/stress ball rolling down the hill. It picked up speed the next week when – surprise! – I had three neglected newspapers.

After the fifth week, I threw away the first two papers. Somewhere around the eighth week, my husband suggested (strongly) I stop the subscription. I couldn't really argue. Even at the height of my coupon zeal I'd used maybe one-fifth of the offers I'd clipped.

So now I do without. Frugality-wise, it sucks. I'm sure there's a more eloquent way to put that, but the long and short of it is that it sucks. Ignoring a pillar of frugality is embarrassing and frustrating – especially when it seems like a load-bearing one.

It's hard to feel frugal when you don't coupon. Five years after giving up, I still occasionally look longingly at a Sunday edition in the store. I get frustrated when I see a grocery or drugstore deal that figures in an offer "as seen in papers." I'm jealous and wistful when I hear other people crow about coupon coups.

Then I remind myself of the stack of newspapers, silently accusing me whenever I glanced their way. I remember the plastic pages full of deals that I'd clipped and never used. I ask myself if a new attempt would end any differently. Since the answer is always a resounding "no," I move on.

Of course, I'm sure there are depressive who are masterminds of scissoring up the Sunday deals and actually matching them with grocery and drugstore sales. I tip my hat to you. As for the rest of you, consider skipping those ads.

But that's not to say you have to give up on coupons entirely. There are easier ways to do it – and they won't leave newsprint all over your hands.

Grocery e-coupons

If you browse grocery ads online you'll see options to add coupons directly onto your shopper loyalty card. One click, and the discount is automatically applied at checkout.

There's nothing to forget at home. E-coupons don't clutter up the place. And they're applied automatically, which means you don't even run the risk of forgetting to hand them to the cashier.

Coupons.com

If you're okay with small batches of paper coupons, use sites like Coupons.com. You just click on the offer you want and print out the result. You do, however, have to remember to bring them with you and hand them to the cashier.

Frugal tip: Go through Swagbucks to get a bonus per coupon redeemed. It works out to about 11 cents per coupon.

Your support network

Ask friends and family for help. Tell them what brands you use often and ask them to send you coupons from their own newspaper subscriptions. My mom sent me Scrubbing Bubbles coupons for years until I switched to another brand. She still sends us Outback coupons, knowing that my husband loves those steak-and-lobster combos.

Your support network wants to support you (it's right there in the name), but there are few concrete ways for them to do that. This option provides an easy way for them to help.

If you must coupon

If you won't be dissuaded from the Sunday ads, be very, very selective as to which ones you choose. Clip only the offers you know you'll use – that is, for products and brands you already know and like. Cutting down on the volume may help you feel less overwhelmed.

You can also use coupon websites that match coupons to sales in supermarkets and drugstores. (CouponMom is a good one, and it's free.) However, these are mainly set up for coupon mavens. Don't get carried away in your attempts, or compare yourself to avid deal seekers who are getting tons of freebies.

I would still suggest tackling regular coupons only if they've already proven not to be an issue for you in the past or if you've got the e-coupons down pat and are looking for more of a challenge.

One last tip

Since you won't be dealing with a lot of coupons, I suggest keeping the ones you have in your wallet. Discounts do you no good if you're at the grocery store while they're still under a magnet on the fridge. Ask me how I know.

Chapter 6: Stocking up

As you know, depressives have good and bad spells. In order to prepare for your bad days you need to stock up on the good ones. The last thing you want is to be stuck at home, staring at the last few squares of toilet paper.

Thus it's important to keep a cache of the items you use most. I know that some people don't have a lot of space to stash extras, but you need to make room – even if that means that packages of toilet paper are stacked somewhere in your living room.

For years my husband drank copious amounts of Mountain Dew. We'd wait for a ridiculous sale, then buy out the store. Limited cupboard space meant that we had to get creative with storage. By "creative" I mean we had about 6 rows of two-liter bottles beside the couch. But every time we opened a 79-cent bottle ($1.99 retail), we cared a little less about what visitors thought.

Forget sale etiquette

Apparently, it's considered rude to clear out a store of a specific sale item. I've never subscribed to this theory.

I may not be able to hit the next sale. The majority of other grocery shoppers will. And they're almost certainly able to visit another store. As far as I'm concerned, my mental and physical health trumps their potential inconvenience.

Besides, most stores have more inventory than what's on the shelves. After you buy them out, they'll restock. In fact, a drugstore manager once confided in my mom that he holds back a certain number of each sale item. Once the sales/coupon mavens have scavenged the shelves, he restocks to give everyone else a shot at the discounts.

That's an important lesson: If you don't see enough of an item on the shelf, ask if they have any in back. If not, most grocery stores will offer rain checks good for at least 30 days. Even if you don't end up using them, at least you have the option.

If you can't use the rain check by its expiration date, go up to the customer service counter and tell them a chronic health condition prevented you from shopping. There's a chance you'll get an extension. (Tip: Some stores will rewrite rain checks just before they expire. Ask about your own supermarket's policy.)

Sale cycles

Frugality experts advise creating a price book for the items you use most. Shoppers carry the notebook or binder with them and compare the current cost to historical trends. This lets them stock up when it'll cost them the least.

Good idea, but I think it's a little too much to ask of most depressives. Instead just try to pay attention to the weekly ads (whether or not you actually go to the store). You'll find that certain sales prices are cyclical. You can probably get a general feel for the price trends without charting them on out paper.

Usually the cycles are four to six weeks, depending on the item in question. You'll also find that there are different degrees of sales.

For example, I've noticed (without graph paper) that my husband's favorite cereal seems to be on a six- to eight-week cycle:

- Full price ($4.59) for one to two weeks of the cycle

- $2.50 for two to three weeks of the cycle.
- $1.99 for one to two weeks of the cycle
- $1.49 (when bought in multiples of six) for one week.

Once you have an idea of trends, you'll be able to make an educated guess about the optimal times to stock up on your favorite nonperishables. When we see the cereal for $1.49 we'll get 12 or more. Ideally, one of us will go back a second time before the sale ends. But as always, we don't beat ourselves up too much if we can't manage it.

It's times like this that a stock-up fund is a budgeter's best friend. You can load up on your favorite items without killing your grocery spending for the month. It gives you peace of mind even when you have to plunk down a bunch of cash to get a great price.

Suboptimal stockups

Unfortunately, you might not be able to get to the store while the best sale is going on. That's why it helps to get an idea of the various price points.

When we run out of cereal before the next $1.49-a-box opportunity (a not-uncommon occurrence thanks to bad spells and/or poor planning) I need to know how much we should buy at the current price.

If we're looking at full-priced boxes, we buy just one or two – enough to get us through until Wednesday, when the grocery store sales change. With luck, the price will then drop to at least $2.50 a box.

If it does, we buy around two weeks' worth. If the prices go down further the next week, we buy as many as possible. Conversely, if they stay the same we'll go in for another two weeks' worth. Either way, it helps ensure that we rarely pay full price.

This is important: ***Sometimes frugality is a matter of degree***. Healthy frugal people can stalk the sales and pounce only on the best prices. That's because they can reliably make it to the grocery store. Heck, they might be able to load up at *multiple* grocery stores.

Depressives can't guarantee they'll be able to go to the store at all. It's dangerous for us to ignore a current sale price in hopes of getting a better one. It could backfire and have us paying full price instead.

In the end it's better to pay $2.50 a box, maybe losing out on $1-per-box savings, than to fork over $4.59 and definitely lose out on $2-per-box savings.

Really suboptimal stockups

Then there are times when you'll have to go against every frugal impulse and stock up at actual retail prices.

Sometimes we can see bad spells coming. It might be that you've been having a really good period, and you can feel that it's about to end. Or maybe you know that a major stressor is coming your way, one which will affect your ability to function. Perhaps you just have a very temporary reprieve during a particularly bad time.

In those cases it's important to stock up on the items you use most, regardless of price. After all, food at retail prices is still cheaper than most food delivery options. And it's almost always cheaper than buying items at a convenience store or drugstore, which could happen if you can't handle a trip to the supermarket.

More to the point, bad spells are hard enough without worrying about running out of cereal/toothpaste/contact lens solution/toilet paper. Besides, if it's a non-perishable you can stock up at sales prices later, which helps even out your per-unit cost in the long run.

Chapter 7: Shop online

Shopping online is great money saver for anyone. But it's also a sanity saver for depressives.

The advantages

The best part about shopping online is that the stuff comes to you. Leaving the house can take huge amounts of energy on bad days (assuming it's possible at all). So why not make things easier? Hop on the computer and get what you need.

Another benefit: a plethora of virtual coupons. You can get the same items that you would at the grocery or drugstore and still enjoy manufacturer's coupons. Sites like Drugstore.com and Soap.com offer brand-specific coupons like you'd find in the dreaded Sunday papers. You might also stumble on additional discounts that you wouldn't get in a brick-and-mortar store.

Cash back sites

Even better: Some of the stores you'll shop at are accessible through cash back sites. That means coupons *and* money back on items you'd buy anyway.

Cash back shopping might sound intimidating, but it's really quite simple. Instead of going directly to the store's website, you:

- Go to the cash back site
- Find the store you want on that site
- Click the store link

The link will take you to the store's website, and you can make your purchase just like you normally do.

(Note: You don't even have to worry about privacy. The only order information the store shares is the order number and how much you spent. Once the cash back site gets those details, it posts the rebate to your account.)

Rebates sites work with more than 2,000 retailers, so you'll almost certainly find your favorite stores on there. Don't believe me? Throughout the book, I'm putting an asterisk by the name of any company that works with cash back sites. I think you'll be surprised.

Once you realize how much money you could save, you just need to choose what rebates site(s) to join. I use several, which allows me to find the highest rate for my particular purchase.

Of course, that might be too much for some people. If the idea of comparison-shopping percentages is daunting, just choose one site and use it for everything. I recommend Mr. Rebates, Ebates, and/or Dollar Dig.

Amazon

Amazon* is bound to come up when discussing online shopping. The site has just about anything you need, generally at prices that are as good as (or better than) other e-stores. It can also get you items faster than most competitors.

For that reason, I recommend people get Amazon Prime – one way or another.

Ideally you have a family member with this service who can add you to his or her Amazon Household. If that's not an option, see if someone wants to split the cost. Half the cost, all the benefits.

The only caveat is that you both need to *really* trust each other. Amazon Household members have to "share" the wallet. That is, you can have your own debit or credit cards on file but you'll each be able to see the other's card information.

Amazon Student is another cheap option. You need to be taking at least one college course and have an email address ending in ".edu." If you meet those requirements, you can get a six-month free trial. After that, you'll pay $49 a year and get all the same benefits as a regular Prime membership.

Otherwise it's best to just pay the full $99. Yes, it sounds a big number but it's really only $8.25 a month. That's $0.26 more than Hulu's monthly cost, whereas Amazon Prime gives you the same streaming benefit plus free two-day shipping with no minimum purchase amount.

That said, keep your eye out for discounts around Golden Globe and Emmy season. Amazon has dropped the cost before when its shows won awards.

If you're not sure whether Prime is worth it, take advantage of a 30-day free trial of Amazon Prime. Just make sure you mark that calendar with reminders to cancel!

One more benefit of Amazon:* If you put off the purchase too long and need the item stat, you can pay a surcharge for same-day or one-day shipping. (Other stores have these options, but at *much* higher rates.)

It's true that an extra $4 to $7 isn't ideal, but remember that you're probably getting a lower price on Amazon anyway and that helps make up for the fee. Besides, we're not going for perfect here. We're going for realistic. Pay a little extra if you must.

Chapter 8: Automate, automate, automate (and then automate some more)

Automatic *anything* is going to be your best friend. Automating is a great way to avoid the stress from bill due dates or the worry of running out of a particular household item.

Bills

First and foremost, automate every bill possible. That's your Internet, utilities, cell phone, insurance premiums and any other item with a due date. Each deadline avoided means more mental energy toward positive endeavors like cooking, hitting sales or just taking care of yourself.

I recommend putting them on a credit card so that you don't have to worry whether you have sufficient funds in your bank account. Besides, if you put them on a rewards card, you get a secondary benefit by using a rewards card.

Auto-refills

Don't just automate bills. Set up automatic shipments of items you use all the time. Amazon offers a 5% discount if you set up recurring shipments of one item. Five or more will get you 15% off. (If any of those items are diapers, I suggest getting Amazon Family: all the features of Amazon Prime plus 20% off diaper subscriptions.)

True, Amazon* won't *always* have the best price. Sometimes I can get better prices at supermarket – but only if I'm able to get to the store. That's never guaranteed. As noted in the Stocking Up section, less-than-optimal savings are better than no savings at all.

Incidentally, it's not just Amazon* that offers discounts. Drugstores, beauty companies, discount retailers like Target,* and so, *so* many more stores have begun to offer 5% to 10% off for auto-refills.

Make a list of the items you buy regularly – especially the ones you always seem to be running out of – and check sites like Target,* Walgreens,* Amazon,* Drugstore.com* and Soap.com* to see whether there's a discount option for auto-delivery. Even if there's no price break, consider signing up for auto-refills anyway. The relief of scheduled deliveries is more than worth it.

Mail-order pharmacy

Whenever possible, take advantage of your insurance's mail-order pharmacy option. This has multiple benefits.

You'll get three months' worth of medications at a time, which means less worry about refills. Some of them let you set up automatic shipments so that you don't even need to remember to reorder. Companies without that feature will still let you manage your account online, and requesting a refill with a click of a button is simpler than a phone call or in-person visit.

Best of all: It's cheaper. One of my husband's medications is $83 for a 30-day supply in the store vs. $101 for a 90-day supply by mail.

Bank

I highly recommend setting up alerts on your bank account. You'll be notified about a low balance, which prevents overdrafting and associated fees. If you have a credit card you can set alerts to remind you when the payment is due.

You can also automate savings. Suppose you have $25 a week transferred into a savings account. That's $100 a month that you're saving without even trying. (Tip: Make sure your balance alert is set to at least $50, so the weekly withdrawal won't cause you to overdraft.)

Chapter 9: Food

Not all depressives have this problem, but food is a huge stressor for me.

For whatever reason, I find that worrying about what to eat is emotionally exhausting. Cooking is even more untenable.

Our frugal faux pas

Except for an occasional pot of spaghetti or rice and beans, Tim and I don't cook. My chronic fatigue makes it hard to rationalize using what little energy I have to prepare food. Even when I do have the energy, depression often makes the proposition seem horribly overwhelming.

As for my Tim:

- Severe asthma can be exacerbated by spices and other ingredient particles in the air.
- Severe, body-wide eczema means food spilled/spitting onto cracked, open skin.
- Fibromyalgia sometimes makes it painful to stand for more than 10 minutes at a time.
- Severe ADD means he can forget where he is in the recipe, including which ingredients have already been added.

Don't get me wrong: I tried. I'd buy groceries and dust off the slow cooker (sometimes literally), flying high on a smug sense of adulting. Things would go well... for a week or so.

Then I'd have a day where I wasn't able to get going. Instead of starting the food at noon, I'd put it off until 1 p.m. When 1 o'clock rolled around, I'd delay. Suddenly, it was 4 or even 5 p.m. and nothing was cooking.

We'd decide to just get some fast food, and I'd vow to start fresh the next day.

On the second day I felt pressure to get back into the swing of things, lest I spiral back into not cooking. So much was riding on my renewed effort. The sense of urgency would build. That stress made me avoid the kitchen all day, and I'd promise myself that I'd do better the next.

By the third day I'd be utterly freaked out – painfully aware that everything could go to hell if I didn't hop to it. Sometimes, the pressure got me moving. Usually it made me order pizza.

Pretty soon I'd have ingredients going bad in the fridge, and the sight of the slow cooker would make me teary with guilt and frustration. I'd have to accept that yet another attempt had failed. Cue the shame spiral.

Each time, my husband would beg me to stop. He'd point out that the results were invariably the same, and it always caused me extreme distress. Couldn't I just accept that cooking didn't work for me? Couldn't I stop beating myself up?

No, I couldn't. That's because cooking – like couponing – is a pillar of frugality. Not cooking felt like blasphemy. How could I possible consider myself frugal while eating out all the time?

Accepting reality

Eventually, even I had to admit that it was ridiculous to keep beating my head against the (kitchen) wall. I couldn't keep hating myself for something that wasn't going to change.

I'd given it my best effort many, many times. Clearly, my best wasn't good enough. So I moved on – and it's one of the best decisions I could have made.

Yes, I'm embarrassed when I talk to other frugal people who think meal prep is relatively simple. Many of them even batch-cook and have enough provisions laid by to feed an army for a full winter. A lot of them wrinkle their noses at the mere mention of fast food. They talk about how much quicker it is to cook for yourself than to go to a restaurant.

Some of them are even depressives themselves. Others have chronic fatigue and still manage to prepare food at home. But you know what? They're not me. I'm sure I can manage things that they can't – which is what I tell myself when the negative thoughts start to creep in.

How we afford it

So how do we manage to not cook *and* keep the food budget in check? We don't. At least, not well.

There are families of four that spend less per month on food than we do. From what I've gathered, most couples who are even remotely frugal spend about half what we do.

But it's no use dwelling on things I can't change. Instead, I try to save as much as possible in this less-than-perfect situation.

Fast food/delivery

Fast food is fine, but we try not to eat it too often. It costs too much, and there are no leftovers. Depending on the restaurant, two value meals will run us $12 to $15. We try to share fries so that we only have to get one value meal and one sandwich; even so, feeding the two of us costs at least $10.

On the other hand, two pizzas ($23 including tip) will provide about three meals each. We get four or five meals each out of delivery from a local Chinese restaurant ($33 after tip). It's the best of both worlds: We don't have to leave the house and we don't have to worry about dinner for a couple of nights.

You can save on delivery fees and tips (at least $5 at a time) if you're okay picking up the food in person. Now that so many restaurants offer online ordering, you can order on your phone and pick up the meal on your way home.

Failing that, just keep an eye out for deals and coupons. The deals we've enjoyed in the past:

- Domino's – Two (or more) for $5.99 each: two-topping medium pizza, oven baked sandwich, chicken, stuffed cheesy bread, pasta, brownies
- Pizza Hut – Any two medium pizzas for $6.99 each
- Pizza Hut – $11 for any medium or large pizza
- Pizza Hut – Two (or more) for $5 each: medium one-topping pizza, two orders of breadsticks/flavor sticks, six-piece wings, pasta, brownie, cookie
- Papa John's – $9.99 for any large pizza

Note: Pizza Hut will send you a survey a couple of days after your order. Fill it out to get a $10 off $20 coupon. You can't use it in conjunction with other specials, but it's still a huge discount.

You might also want to look into the Entertainment Book. The coupons – usually buy one get one free – help if you eat at enough fast food and pizza places. It's great for couples. Depending on what the food is, single people could get both and eat the other one later. (I've seen hamburgers revived in the microwave. I don't recommend it.)

Convenience food

For quite a while we ate a lot of fast food. Two people, one to two meals a day, proved to be too expensive even by my newly lax budgetary standards. All the sodium wasn't great for my blood pressure either.

That's when I started stocking up on convenience food.

Let me start by saying that the best thing you can do is get used to eating the same thing over and over. If you can manage that at least 80% of the time, life will be much easier (and cheaper).

I subsist mainly on protein bars, peanut butter toast and Healthy Choice frozen meals. No, you don't have to be *this* boring. For me, it's what works because I'm watching my calories and because I hate having too many food choices.

I have a protein bar first thing in the morning. Two or three hours later, I have some peanut butter toast. A couple of hours after that, more toast. Two hours later, a frozen meal or, if I'm feeling really disinterested, more toast. I have a frozen meal for dinner, and a protein bar in the evening.

All in all, my food costs around $5 a day. Far from ideal, but a lot better than $6 to $7 per meal at a fast-food joint.

I still have fast food from time to time but a lot less of it. Better for me, better for our budget. Besides, sometimes just choosing a fast food restaurant stresses me out. I have no idea why, but I've accepted it and moved on.

Tim has cereal for one or two meals a day. Then he only has to worry about dinner, which is usually fast food or pizza.

Variety is the spice of life

Like I said, you don't have to be as boring as we are. There are plenty of ways to have more variety in your diet without cooking.

Frozen entrees/dinners: We're not just talking about dry steak and limp vegetables. These days there's a range of cuisines and food types, including vegetarian, vegan and gluten-free. Most go on sale for $2 to $3. Even at $4, it's cheaper (and probably healthier) than fast food.

Frozen pizzas: 'Nuff said.

Sandwiches: Sandwiches don't have to be fancy. All you need are cold cuts, cheese and some bread. You can throw them in the microwave for a hot sandwich or just eat them cold. Lettuce and tomato, while nice, are utterly optional. Don't forget about the old standby: peanut butter and jelly.

Spaghetti: It's not the most nutritious meal in the world, but it *is* cheap and easy. Choose noodles with added fiber to feel full longer. If you want to get fancy, you can buy prefab meatballs at the supermarket to simmer in the sauce.

Canned soup: Quick and easy, whether you heat it up in the microwave or actually go to the trouble of using the stove.

Canned chili: Also quick, also easy. My husband throws in barbecue sauce and salsa. It's surprisingly delicious.

Mac and cheese: Frozen or out of a box, it's great comfort food.

Oatmeal: No one wants a lot of fuss in the morning. This is very nutritious, very filling and, most importantly, easy. If you can't handle dealing with a saucepan, make it in the microwave (five minutes at 50% power) or just buy instant.

Cold cereal: Delicious *and* fine for any meal.

Bagels and cream cheese: Also good for any meal.

Rice and beans: This one is a bit of a cheat: You have to make a cup of rice. Put it in a bowl and add salsa, a drained can of beans, maybe some corn and however much red pepper, black pepper and garlic you want. Stir until it's all mixed up, and eat it alone, with corn chips or wrapped in a tortilla.

If you can cook

If you're okay with small amounts of cooking, you should focus on what my mom affectionately calls "one-pot glop." That is, anything that can be made in one large pot or in a slow cooker.

I grew up on minestrone, beef stew, bean soup, spaghetti (sauce made in the slow cooker), sloppy joes and chili.

For slow cooker recipes, check out the blog 365 Days of Slow Cooking. Stephanie O'Dea made at least one item in a crock pot each day for a year. She's also written a number of cookbooks, but I recommend starting with the free option.

Slow cookers are great because you can set them when you leave for work. By the time you get home, there's a meal waiting.

Marinades are also your friend. Let the marinade soak in for an hour – or leave the meat in a bag overnight – and you have a fresh flavor without worrying about ingredients.

Another good option is Erin Chase's FreezEasy meals. They're cheap, every step is laid out and you can prepare 10 meals in one hour.

The plan comes with a grocery list of all the ingredients – grouped by store section to make it extra easy. You watch the assembly video to prepare each one. At the end of the hour, you'll have 10 meals in resealable bags. (Printable labels are provided, too.)

Freeze the bags until you need a meal. When you do, pick one out and submerge it in warm water for half an hour or, if you have more time, thaw it in the fridge overnight. Once thawed, you can throw the contents into a pot, pan or slow cooker, and you'll have a meal.

She has five plans: all chicken, all beef, all pork, trio of meats and combo. Each is only $7, and you can get all five for $25.

I'll be honest, though: Even something this simple isn't for me. So don't feel bad if you're not up for it. Still, if you *can* manage small amounts of cooking, this could make your life a lot easier. And at $7, it isn't exactly a huge fiscal risk.

Chapter 10: Gift cards

Since you're going to eat out more, it's a good idea to ask for fast food, pizza and restaurant gift cards for birthdays and holidays. Obviously, if you have something specific you need or want, focus on that. Otherwise, this is a great way to help ease the cost of convenience food.

Meanwhile, you don't have to wait for other people to give you gift cards. There are a slew of websites selling discounted GCs. Use sites like GiftCardGranny for a quick way to compare the discounts. Even better, you can earn rewards points toward free GCs.

Remember that gift cards aren't just for restaurants or clothing stores. You can save money in all sectors of life: gas, groceries, coffee, fast food, movie theaters, video games, club stores, kids' and baby items, technology, home improvement and more. Combine discounted GCs with a store's sale, and you can really clean up!

If you (or a family member) belong to a club store, you'll find GCs discounted up to 30%. Costco has movie passes, gym memberships, Nutrisystem,* Build-A-Bear,* Peet's Coffee, See's Candies,* ColdStone Creamery and numerous restaurants. Sam's Club* has most of those, plus iTunes, Google Play, Disney* and more.

However, you need to make sure you don't spend it just because it's there. For example, if you have a Red Robin gift card you might choose to go there more often because the money's already paid out. It feels free, but it isn't: That's *your* money on the card.

Remind yourself it's a discount for future spending, not a license to spend freely.

One more thing: Guard your cards! If you lose them in the house, you'll be frustrated (and out the money). If you lose them outside the house, someone else will go shopping on your dime.

Chapter 11: Comfort spending

Frugality is about purposeful, meaningful spending to make sure that you get the most value out of each dollar. One of the biggest roadblocks to that is the dreaded impulse purchase.

Most people buy themselves a little something because they feel like they're worth it. Depressives, on the other hand, are probably more prone to buying things because they *don't* think they're worth it. They feel worthless, so they seek comfort.

Everyone has created an association between at least one product and feeling comforted. It's even easier for depressives, since we're more often prone to sadness and, therefore, the need for comfort. This means we're even more at risk for the financial deathtrap of comfort spending, be it food, the latest technology or other indulgences.

It's never good to buy on impulse, but what makes it dangerous is that so many of the purchases are small.

It's easy to remember when you spent a bunch of money on something that ended up not being worth it. You'll probably factor that into your decision for the next big purchase.

But inexpensive items don't register as well. Are you going to remember that the $2 candy didn't actually help last time? Or are you just going to focus on how $2 really isn't that much and just how badly you think you need that chocolate right now?

Don't get me wrong: I'm not going to say that chocolate doesn't make you feel better. (Though I always feel worse once I realize *how much* chocolate it took to lift my mood.) But you have to look critically at the cost/benefit ratio.

Comfort food

Evaluating the merits of comfort food can be difficult. Immediacy makes things feel far more valuable than they really are. When you've had a bad day and are staring at the ice cream section of the grocery store, Ben & Jerry's might feel a lot more valuable than a goal for the future.

And you know what? Sometimes it is. Sometimes comfort food is exactly what we need to make a day better. In that case, it's money well spent. More often it's just a temporary balm, gone long before the problem is resolved. (Unless the problem is that you hadn't had ice cream in ages.)

So how do you tell the difference? Well, it's tough. The best two questions to ask are:

- How well did this work in the past?
- How will I feel once the food is gone?

In the past, were you left with a stomachache or a better disposition? Were you left regretting the calories and spent cash? Or did you cheer up enough to tackle the problem?

And if you indulge now, what will have changed? Will the deadline be more manageable? Will whatever is stressing you out still be there? What about the depressive episode? How will the comfort food help that?

Again, sometimes it really will. Sometimes a meal at a sit-down restaurant makes me feel like I can take on the world. And when I have a cold, hot and sour soup always makes me feel taken care of.

There can absolutely be value in comfort food, but it can also be a waste of money. The trick is learning to distinguish between the two scenarios – and being okay with the fact that you'll probably get it wrong sometimes.

Comfort distraction

Of course, some people *don't* eat their feelings like I do. Instead they prefer to escape from reality for a little while: a movie, a night out, a spa treatment, etc. Alas, that kind of stuff adds up fast.

Once again you need to ask yourself whether this worked in the past and whether you'll feel any better when it's over. Sure, a movie will keep you occupied for a couple of hours but then you'll be back in the real world, at least $10 poorer. Yes, a facial, pedicure, manicure or massage might relax you. But is it a temporary reprieve, or will it actually make a difference?

Don't get me wrong: Sometimes the distraction is worth the money. Only you can decide that, and again, there's a decent chance that you'll be wrong a few times. The best you can do is to focus on previous experiences and your best judgment.

If you're sure you need *some* form of distraction, here are a few frugal workarounds:

Movies

Try renting a Redbox movie instead of going to the theater. If you can't stand to be in your house another minute, see if any friends want to watch it at their place. Redbox usually releases at least one free code a month, so you might not have to spend anything at all.

If you want the full movie theater experience, try a second-run house. This is where films go after they leave the main theaters but before the DVDs are released. Their admission is usually around $3, and some have half-price days.

And if you really want to see a movie only out in regular theaters? Buy a discounted gift card for the theater chain. (Note: You can buy electronic gift cards for use online or at the ticket window.)

Food and drink

If you're more in the mood for drinks, make sure you know the happy hour specials near your home and work.

Find good happy hour guides by visiting Yelp, setting it to your town and typing in "happy hour." Or Google "[your city] best happy hours." Take notes for future reference. Make sure you set yourself a drink and/or price limit ahead of time. Do your best to stick to it, even when the buzz sets in.

Don't forget to pick a place with food specials, too. Most people get the munchies when they drink, and you don't want to be tempted by full-price fare.

Speaking of eating: Check out local cooking schools. There's one near me with three-course meals (plus a non-alcoholic drink) for $12 to $19. We're talking high-end recipes, folks.

Spa services

When the stress hits or you're really glum, you might be tempted by spa services: massages, pedicures, manicures and facials. These are a great way to pamper yourself – but not your wallet.

Once again, you need to ask yourself how much the service will really help. Will nicely painted toenails actually change anything? Maybe taking care of yourself will give you a new outlook on the world. Or maybe you'll just have softer, more attractive feet while curled up on the couch, feeling overwhelmed.

We all know that most of these services are more likely to leave your wallet lighter than your spirits. Still, if you're convinced that one of these treatments is just the thing you need, be sure to look into frugal versions.

Beauty schools tend to offer very affordable manicures and pedicures. Almost all of them will have the option for a facial, usually for $25 or less. This can be a great way to pamper yourself while simultaneously cushioning your wallet.

Not comfortable with a beauty school undergrad? Then check out social buying sites like Groupon* or LivingSocial.* You should be able to find facials for under $30.

You can also find affordable massages at massage schools, where a 50-minute session will run you about $30. That said, it's not much more to get a professional massage through the social buying sites. (Though you probably don't have to tip the students.)

Retail therapy

Some people shop to comfort themselves. It's true that there can be an initial rush of excitement over a snazzy new shirt or a brilliant piece of technology. But that rush will fade. Then you're left with the bill, which can be depressing in its own right.

So how do you avoid impulse buys?

Walk away

The best thing you can do is to get some space between you and the item.

Sometimes we get so wrapped up in comparing and contrasting, it can start to feel like a purchase is inevitable rather than optional. Walking away to clear your head may make you realize you can hold off on the purchase. If you do end up buying it, at least you'll be certain you really want it.

If possible, it's best to delay the purchase for one to two days. This gives you time to see if other options exist. Perhaps one of your friends will loan or give you something similar, or maybe you don't really need it at all. If you're still thinking about the item two days later, it's more likely to be a purchase you won't regret.

That said, depressives can't always be sure when they'll be able to come back. It makes delaying less tenable. But you still have options.

- Walk away for at least half an hour. Find something to distract yourself for a bit so that your head is clearer when you reconsider the purchase.
- See if the store has a website. If so, you can walk away and still make the purchase later. (Bonus: The store may be on a cash back site!)

Focus on the future

Another good deterrent is to always have a reminder of your other goals with you. Again, immediacy is the enemy. What's a vacation months from now compared with a warm latte on a cold day? Yeah, a house is great, but you *really* believe that you'll watch this DVD over and over.

You need to make sure long-term goals feel more pressing. Write your current debt total on a sticky note and slap that bad boy on your credit/debit card. Saving for a vacation or down payment? Print out a small picture of a plane, landmark or house, then tape it to the inside of your wallet or wrap it around the card. Each time you spend, you're coming face-to-face with your other objectives.

Clothes shopping? Use your phone to take a picture of your closet. You probably won't buy as much when you can see how many clothes you already have. This also ensures you won't buy something and then find that you already have an almost identical item at home.

It may help to have pictures of other clutter in your house: bookcases, gadget charging stations, etc. When you're tempted to buy something, ask yourself where you'd fit it. And no, you don't get to cheat by spending money on organizers just to make more space!

Talk it over – with yourself

Usually we're tempted to buy because an item promises solutions: a faster phone charge, a better-organized home, a kitchen implement to make food prep easier. But is it really worthwhile? Here are a few questions to ask yourself:

1. "Did I know I needed this solution before I saw it?" If you've never said, "Gosh, I would *absolutely* eat mashed potatoes if I only had a self-propelling masher" then you don't need one.

2. "How often do I encounter this problem?" If you only have to shuffle gadgets around a crowded charging port once a week, it's not really worth paying for a solution.
3. "How big a headache is the problem?" If it's a minor inconvenience, then it's probably not worth the money.

I'm not saying that the answer will always be negative. Sometimes there are items that are worth every penny.

I once spent $17 (1990s dollars, no less) on a garlic roller for my mom. The gadget peeled the clove with a few quick rolls – a substantial improvement on our method, which involved knives and swear words. Was the item necessary? No. But it *was* an awesome labor-saving device that was used frequently. All in all, a good buy.

So that's really the ultimate question: Is this item going to help with something that's already a part of your life, or are you buying it to get the ball rolling? Because the latter rarely works out.

An elliptical machine won't make you start exercising, but it may be a good buy for someone who already religiously uses one at the gym.

A special peeler/corer won't make you eat more pineapple – ask me how I know – but it's great for people who already regularly deal with the hassle.

Spending when you're already comfortable

Of course, comfort spending isn't always about making yourself feel better. Sometimes you spend more *because* you finally feel good.

It can be easy to overspend during a reprieve from a bad spell. You don't feel worthless anymore, which means you're finally worth spending some money on, right?

Or you're just so excited to feel good that you want to get out of the house and do... everything! You want to go out with friends. You want to catch up on the latest movies. You want to go on a couple of dates. And you want some nice new clothes to do it all in.

Once again, it's about making conscious choices about value in spending. Think purchases through as best you can. Spending limits could also help keep you from getting carried away in the thrill of actually wanting to be out and about.

The trade-off

In the end, you need to remember that the money for your indulgence has to come from somewhere. Try using if/then statements to get more perspective:

If I buy this $50 dress, then I can't replace my shoes that are wearing out.

If I go to this $10 movie, I can't eat any meals out this week.

If I buy this $5 coffee, then I can't have that $5 happy hour drink with friends. Which will help my frustrations more: venti or venting?

Sometimes the trade-off is worth it. What matters is that you ask the question and really *think* about your answer. Informed choices are the best route to frugality. Well, that and forgoing movie theater popcorn.

Chapter 12: Avoid the library

Frugal articles abound on the awesomeness of public libraries. Why, you can get magazines and movies as well as books! Phoenix libraries let you borrow free passes to museums, botanical gardens and other city attractions. Depending on where you live, you might be able to borrow art, toys and even fishing rods.

Libraries are absolutely wonderful resources that should be fully taken advantage of – by healthy people. Depressives, on the other hand, may find free public libraries very expensive.

Most libraries have late fees of 10 to 20 cents per book per day. Thanks to bad spells and my husband taking out as many as 15 graphic novels at a time, our combined book borrowing often cost $5-10.

Even writing down the due date on the calendar was iffy at best. Knowing that the deadline was coming up sometimes just generated stress, which made it harder to get the books back.

Eventually, I declared no more libraries. That is, no more *physical* ones. We now use the Phoenix Digital Library. Once your borrowing period is up, the book is automatically returned. While not every book is available in digital form, we can still choose from a huge selection of both regular and audiobooks.

A ton of other free e-book options exist. Gizmo's freeware site lists more than 900 sites for free e-books, sorted by genre. It also has 224 places to find free audiobooks.

Or check out Open Library's more than 1.6 million titles, dating back as far as 1008. Project Gutenberg offers more than 45,000 e-books. Google Play has more than 4 million titles, many of which are free. ManyBooks.net has more than 29,000 e-books, and you can filter them by genre.

And of course, if you do have Amazon Prime, you'll get access to half a million free e-books. You can also get Kindle Unlimited, which has a million e-books and thousands of audiobooks. (But first give it a test run with a 30-day free trial.)

Chapter 13: Cancel the gym membership

Some people can work out only if they join a gym. The fact that their money is wasted if they don't, in fact, exercise keeps them motivated.

The rest of us, depressed and healthy alike, tend to find the financial angle more intimidating than motivating. The moment our attendance falters, the stress of wasted money sets in. The more pressure, the harder it is to start up again.

The frustration and guilt build until you've spent hundreds of dollars on a building you rarely visit. Think about it: No gym could function on just the membership dues of the hundred (or fewer) people you spot in your various gym trips. For every person who checks in, no doubt dozens more stay away.

If even mentally healthy people find gym attendance so hard, what hope do most depressives have?

It's especially frustrating since it's believed that exercise can ease depression. Low serotonin levels cause – or at least correlate to – depression. Exercise increases the production of serotonin. So it's important for depressives to find some way to work out.

Ideally, that would be for at least 30 minutes a day. But this book isn't about ideals. Medical professionals believe that as little as five minutes of exercise can help boost mood.

So frugal-leaning depressives need to find an affordable way to work out that doesn't include a gym.

There's the obvious suggestion of walking or jogging outside. Unfortunately, leaving the house can be half the battle. That's why at-home exercise may be the best option.

YouTube has a surprising number of free exercise videos. I personally like Xhit for strength-training because the videos are generally 8-12 minutes.

As someone with chronic fatigue, I find these short videos are a good entry into workouts. Even as a depressive, I find it's a lot harder to say "I'm not up for an eight-minute video" than to demur on 20 to 30 minutes of exercise. Once I could reliably do one video a day, I worked my way up to doing two in a row.

Some of the workouts don't include dumbbells; but if you prefer ones that do, you can choose to make your own weights:

- Use cans of food (the weight is right on the label!)
- Fill an empty water bottle: 20 ounces for 1.3 pounds, a liter for 2.2 pounds
- Fill a bag (or water bottle) with sand

Once you're sure you'll keep working out, you can always buy some real dumbbells. (Frugal tip: Watch for them on Freecycle, or put up your own "wanted" request there.)

Xhit has cardio workouts, too, but I don't like those as much. Instead I use "walk at home" videos on Leslie Sansone's YouTube channel. Some of them are just one-mile walks, which are good for those starting out.

Amazon Prime Video also has workouts you can watch for free. I don't have access to the service, so I can't make any specific suggestions. Still, the titles I saw listed looked promising.

Bonus: Instructors in workout videos can't hear you yell and/or swear at them. (*See? Doesn't that feel good?* "No, Leslie, it's awful! No one likes exercise! What's wrong with you?!")

All of that being said, some depressives may find the gym motivating. If that's the only way you can make yourself work out, then don't cancel your membership.

As always, frugality isn't just about saving money; it's also about getting value out of what you do spend. And there's very little in this world more valuable than your health.

Chapter 14: Get rid of cable (probably)

There is absolutely a chance that you're one of the few people who actually should keep your cable or satellite. It's just not a very *big* chance.

I put off cutting the cord for years. My husband and I are both home all day and our combined health issues mean we spend most nights in. I truly believed that we needed cable's vast array of choices.

Then our bill hit $100. (We were subsidizing my in-laws in our guest house, which is what pushed our bill up so high.) There was no way I was going to pay that much for the second-lowest Dish package.

I started researching Hulu, making a list of the shows we watched and comparing it to what we'd get with the streaming service. Between that and Netflix (which we already had) we would lose only two programs plus my beloved "Law & Order" reruns. For a $92 savings, I could live without all three.

That was almost three years ago, and we've saved more than $2,500. We can almost always find something to watch, and on the rare occasions that we can't, we opt for a $1.25 movie at Redbox.

Again: *Twenty-five hundred dollars*. Thus my advice: Make a list of all your shows, then review Amazon Prime, Hulu Plus and Netflix. You'll probably be pleasantly surprised.

One big exception, of course, is professional sports. If you're a fan then yes, it may be worthwhile to stick with cable or satellite. Maybe.

If ESPN is the only thing keeping you from taking the leap, consider Sling TV. You'll get 20 channels, including ESPN and ESPN 2, for $20 a month. Just download the app and use it on any device that runs other streaming services.

We're talking huge savings here, guys. Cable or satellite TV customers will, on average, save $408 to $741 a year (depending on what combination of Sling TV, Hulu Plus, Netflix and Amazon Prime they choose). That's up to 88% less than cable or satellite. That kind of money is well worth the half hour it takes to make a list.

Chapter 15: Save on utilities

Utilities will always eat up a good chunk of the budget, especially if you're a homeowner. Most renters at least pay for their electricity. Here are some to help keep your bill down without a lot of extra or daunting effort.

Help with utilities

Let's start with a few resources for low-income people. There are more than you might know.

Your main resource is the Benefits.gov website, which lists all available assistance programs. Note: This site lists *all* programs, so go through it a little bit at a time to keep your eyes from glazing over.

Two programs I'd like to highlight are LifeLine Support and the Low Income Home Energy Assistance Program.

LifeLine Support helps low-income people have phone service, whether that's a discounted landline or free cell phone service. You should qualify if you live below 135% of the federal poverty limit or if you receive benefits like SNAP, Medicaid, TANF, Section 8 and SSI. Find out more at the LifeLine Support website.

The LIHEAP site offers a state-by-state list of resources to help you pay utility bills. These include charities to contact if you're in danger of having your water or power shut off. Check out LIHEAP's State Energy Assistance page for more information.

Now for the rest of you…

Electricity

There's the obvious suggestion of changing your lightbulbs out for compact fluorescent bulbs. CFLs use less energy but provide about the same amount of light as traditional bulbs. They also last longer.

They generally aren't cheap, but they're worth it. Look for periodic specials that stores like Home Depot,* Lowe's,* Sam's Club* and Costco have in conjunction with the local electric company.

Frugal tip: Visit your electric company's website – or call, if the phone doesn't bother you – to ask for an energy savings kit. That usually includes a couple of CFL bulbs.

While you can absolutely change the bulbs out ahead of time, I prefer to just switch them out as the traditional bulbs wear out. Waste not, want not – and *definitely* want-not to shop for bulbs any sooner than necessary.

Be sure you're not leaving lights and/or fans on in rooms after you leave them. This can be especially easy to forget when it comes to bathroom fans. Avoiding mildew is smart, but you probably don't need to run the fan all day.

If you want to take things even further, unplug any electric devices you're not using at the moment, including computers, TVs, modems, microwaves, etc. These items draw small amounts of power even when they're turned off.

Of course, most people find it aggravating to go around the house unplugging items (or plugging them back in). In that case, invest in a few power strips with on/off buttons. Those don't draw power when they're off, so all you have to do is make sure they're in easy to reach locations.

During the day, try to forgo electric light for any direct sunlight you can get. It saves electricity and also helps with mood.

That said, I highly suggest buying a light therapy device to treat Seasonal Affective Disorder. I work from home and don't get the benefit of sun during a daily commute, which means I struggle with SAD. even here in sunny Phoenix.

My light helps me feel more alert. It also curbs some of the worst symptoms of the condition: listlessness, extra depression and a very real danger of death by carbs.

Heating/cooling

One of the biggest components of your electric bill is probably the cost of heating and/or cooling your home. Enough cost-cutting hacks exist that I decided HVAC deserves its own section.

Let me start with a word of caution: Depressives should be particularly careful in this area. Actions that are too extreme could increase issues with inertia. Even healthy people have a hard time leaving the coziness of a warm bed in the winter, and most people get proportionately more lethargic as temperatures rise in summer.

Since many depressives already struggle with lassitude, you'll want to be judicious in raising and lowering the house temperature. Keeping the house colder and snuggling up under a blanket sounds great. However, it makes it much harder to get up to run errands or do chores. The same goes for leaving the comfort of a fan's direct breeze on a hot day.

If the following tips lead to decreased productivity, please reconsider the cost/benefit ratio of a few degrees on the thermostat.

Before you start any of the following changes, make sure vents and doors stay closed in unused rooms. There's no need to heat or cool the guest room until you actually have visitors.

Once you're concentrating your HVAC's output where it matters, look critically at your home's ambient temperature.

Between Phoenix summer temperatures and the fact that we're home all day, our HVAC system works almost constantly five or six months of the year. In the summer, electricity rates nearly double, so we have to work to lower our consumption.

Thus we set the thermostat as high as we can comfortably stand, with ceiling fans for a nice cross breeze. But our main tactic is stripping down to the bare essentials – with an emphasis on "bare." Assuming you don't have roommates, there's really no point in wearing clothes around the house when it's hot out. Your home is your space, after all, and you can be as naked as you like.

In addition to using less electricity, there are two other bonuses:

- If you were fully dressed only for a couple of hours you can wear the clothes again. That means less laundry.
- If you have body-image issues you may find this helps you get more comfortable in your own skin. It certainly helped me.

Depending on how far you take the "strip down" idea, you may want to put down a sheet on the couch or in your favorite chair. Freedom from sartorial strictures doesn't mean you should ignore basic hygiene.

No matter your state of undress, you'll also need a fan. We got ours for about $5 at a Goodwill and my mom found a pedestal fan for $2.50 at a church rummage sale.

Failing that, keep an eye on store ads. Early in the season you can generally find fans on sale for $10 to $15. As the weather gets warmer, it's harder to get them for under $20 or even $25.

You'll want a fan on you whenever possible, including at the foot of your bed at night. (Bonus: This is an affordable white-noise machine.) Box fans can tip, so it's best to put it by a wall or on a chair with a high back.

Some people recommend setting ice cubes in front of the fan for a faux air-conditioning effect but I shy away from it for fear of mildew. You can always try keeping a cool (or even frozen) cloth around your neck. There are self-cooling towels that some people swear by.

So that takes care of the heat section. Now on to my favorite: the cold.

Personally, I prefer dealing with cooler temperatures. After all, you can strip down only so far; but it's easy to add layers until you're warm. So when it comes to cold, I'm all set. Flannel pajama pants are invaluable, as is a comfortable cardigan. Be sure to have a cozy blanket or heated throw on the couch to relax under while you watch TV or read.

My mom sometimes drapes a rice sock around her shoulders while she works or even under the covers at bedtime to warm her icy feet.

Never heard of a rice sock? It's the stingy version of a heating pad. Here are the *incredibly* complex instructions: Put a cup of uncooked rice into a sock; tie a knot in the sock; throw it in the microwave for 30 to 45 seconds. Ta-da!

Or just use a space heater in the room where you spend the most time. They're relatively cheap (starting around $15), and they allow you to keep the rest of your house cool without having to bundle up. A friend with fibromyalgia swears by her heater to keep her achy joints warm in Northern California.

Just be careful not to put it next to flammable items (mail, blankets, pets, etc.) According to the National Fire Protection Association, space heaters accounted for a third of home heating fires and four out of five related fire deaths.

No matter what the season, be sure to give your thermostat a rest when you're not at home. During the winter, that means turning the temperature way down when you leave for work. It wouldn't hurt to turn it down at night too. That's what blankets are for.

During the summer, you'll want to turn the thermostat off (or set the temperature much higher) while you're at work. You can turn it back on as soon as you get home and stand in front of the HVAC vent (or that trusty fan) to cool off.

Homeowners may want to have a programmable thermostat installed. That way you don't have to worry about fiddling with the thermostat before you leave. You can also set it to start warming up or cooling down shortly before you get home. That should make things a lot more comfortable when you walk through the door.

Water

According to Consumer Reports (and contrary to popular wisdom) baths actually use significantly more water than showers. That's important since you're paying for that water twice: water rates coming in and sewer rates going out.

Here are a few ways to use less:

Many cities provide a free low-flow showerhead through their energy efficiency programs. Take advantage! If your town doesn't offer that, buy one. (Renters: You can always take it with you when you move.)

This will cut your water usage by at least 50%, so it's a worthwhile investment. I recommend shopping for one online. You can read other customers' reviews, and you might be able to get cash back.

However, even low-flow heads won't save much water if you take epic showers. Personally, I don't really understand long showers. I grew up in Anchorage, Alaska, which meant that for a good chunk of the year I cleaned up in a very cold house with mediocre-at-best water pressure. I was *very* focused on minimizing the amount of time I was naked, so I learned to take very quick showers:

- Step under the stream to get everything damp enough for the soap.
- Turn around and, while soaping up, tilt your head into the stream of water
- Turn and rinse your body while shampooing
- Lather, rinse, *don't* repeat, and you're done.

If I'm so inclined I can be in and out of the shower in under two minutes. That's still not as water-saving as a "navy shower," in which you get yourself damp, shut off the water, soap up, rinse quickly and jump out.

But not everyone is interested in absolute efficiency in bathing rituals. In that case, try playing music in the shower. It's more fun to shower while belting out your favorite tunes – in fact, it's the only time some people's singing ever sounds good – and the number of songs you hear helps you keep tabs on how long you've been in there. If you're worried about getting water on your phone, invest in a cheap Bluetooth speaker. (They start as low as $5.)

If you live with a significant other, consider sharing a shower. Not only will you save water, but there's someone to wash your back!

Incidentally, low-flow showerheads aren't the only way to slow your water output. You can attach aerators (also called diffusers) to bathroom and kitchen faucets. They generally cost less than $10 and you simply screw them on by hand. You'll still get plenty of water pressure, but you'll be using less each time you turn on the faucet.

The toilet is another major source of higher water bills. Newer models use fewer gallons per flush but not everyone has the option of replacing their current one. In that case, seal a brick in a Ziploc bag and place it in the tank, being careful not to disturb the toilet hardware. Or fill a large soft-drink bottle with pebbles and put it in the tank – again, being careful not to interfere with the toilet workings. Don't worry, there'll still be plenty of water to flush.

If you're willing to take it further, there's the old "if it's yellow let it mellow" routine. I work from home and drink a lot of water – *a lot* of water – so I feel this is necessary. But it's definitely not for everyone, including my husband. This isn't an issue you want to push on people, and it's definitely not a method you should use when you have guests. (Unless they're unwelcome ones.)

Another big part of the water bill can be lawns and gardens. Gardeners and lawn-lovers need to make sure the grass and/or plants have at least a couple of hours to absorb the water before it starts to get hot. It's best to water in the early morning or early evening. Watering during the day can mean you lose a lot to evaporation. For the same reason, you shouldn't bother with oscillating sprinklers.

Some people like to get soil moisture sensors to keep an eye on whether the plants even need watering. After all, too much water can be just as bad as not enough. There's a huge range in price but sensors start as low as $7.

Or get specific about where the water goes. My mom poked holes into soda-bottle bottoms and buried one next to each plant in her small veggie garden. Rather than spray water willy-nilly, she simply filled each bottle and let the liquid seep out to the plants' roots.

Some very eco/money-minded gardeners put a bucket in the shower while they wait for the water to warm up. Others use bathwater for their lawn. Frankly, both would be far too much hassle for me, even if I liked baths *or* gardening. But to each his own.

Phone

If you're content with a landline, I highly recommend Ooma. It's VOIP, which is the same type of service cable companies and Vonage* offer.

To use Ooma, you have to buy a base, called an Ooma Telo (which will run you $70 to $100), but after that you pay only taxes and fees – even on long-distance calls. We switched last spring and our biggest monthly bill has been $4.28. Vonage* was nearly $36 a month.

But some people want a phone that works when the Internet is down, or they can't afford an Internet connection at home. In that case, call your phone company. Ask for the most basic line they have.

Say no to:

- Call waiting (How often do two people you *want* to talk to call simultaneously?)
- Voicemail (Get a phone with an answering machine.)
- Long distance (Get a phone card or a prepaid cell.)

That last one might be a bit controversial. Yes, the phone company's long-distance rates are better. But those better rates come only in packages. The bells and whistles make the "cheap" long distance too expensive.

If you make a lot of long distance calls, then you can reconsider the issue. Most people don't use it enough to justify the cost.

If you stick to the no-frills option, you should pay around $12 to $15 a month for phone service.

Keep in mind, however, that even that low a bill adds up. If you can afford an Internet connection Ooma will have paid for itself within a year. If you can't afford the Ooma Telo maybe it could be a birthday or holiday gift: When family and friends ask what you want, request gift cards to a place where you can buy the unit (Target,* Best Buy,* Amazon,* et al.).

Chapter 16: Cell phone

It's not news that cell phone plans are expensive. Most people I know pay $80 to $100 for an individual plan. Luckily, some companies provide significantly lower prices.

They're able to do this because they rent "space" from larger networks, avoiding costs like cell tower upkeep. The other trick is that these companies don't provide you with a free or significantly discounted phone when you sign up.

Sometimes the service will work with your existing phone, so additional costs will come only if you want to upgrade. If you don't have the right kind of phone, the companies offer cheaper, refurbished units on their websites or you can find a used phone on Craigslist or eBay.* Or put it out in the universe that you're looking for a phone; a friend or relative who's planning to upgrade may pass the old unit along to you.

Here's a look at the most common alternative cell services:

Republic Wireless

This is the company that has most personal finance bloggers raving. Every reviewer I've seen wishes he or she had switched sooner.

Republic has three different plans. All come with unlimited talk and text, so the only difference is data. You can choose 1, 2 or 3 GBs a month for $25, $40 or $55 a month.

The beauty is that you pay only for what you use. Republic will refund you for any unused data. So if you're on the 2 GB plan but only use one, you'll get $15 back in the form of an account credit.

According to Republic Wireless, the average customer bill is $13.12. It's worth noting that most customers seem to be avid WiFi users. They switch to WiFi whenever there's a trusted connection, which keeps data usage – and therefore, the bill – lower.

The main drawback? You can't bring your beloved Apple devices. This plan uses the Moto E and Moto G phones, for $129 and $199 respectively. Yet even iPhone-loving bloggers say the savings makes it worth abandoning iOS. (Tip: You can save substantially by buying directly on the Motorola* website. I found the Moto G on sale there for $99.99.)

Ting

If you don't want to give up your iPhone, Ting may work for you. As long as your phone will work with the Sprint network, it'll be compatible with Ting.

The service is all about paying for what you use:

Minutes: 1-100 ($3), 101-500 ($9), 501-1000 ($18), 1001-2100 ($35), after that 1.9 cents per additional minute

Text: 1-100 ($3), 101-1,000 ($5), 1,001-2,000 ($8), 2,001-4,800 ($11), ¼ cent per additional message

Data (MB): 1-100 ($3), 101-500 ($12), 501-1000 ($19), 1001-2000 ($29),1.5 cents per additional MB

You'll also pay $6 per device each month. To see how much you'd save, get your last couple of cell phone bills and run the numbers on Ting's calculator. That will give you an idea of how much you'd save and, therefore, whether the switch is worthwhile.

Note: If you don't have a Sprint-capable phone you'll need to get one. While that does greatly increase the startup costs, the savings could quickly cover the price of the phone.

Prepaid

If you want to keep things a little simpler, go for a straightforward prepaid plan from companies like Straight Talk,* Boost Mobile,* Tracfone,* Cricket and Virgin. Regular cell companies like AT&T,* Verizon,* T-Mobile* and Sprint* also offer prepaid options.

The plans usually run $45 to $55 for talk, text and data. Generally there's a cap on high-speed data; after the cap the data would run more slowly but still be unlimited.

However, you'll have to pay for your own smartphone. To keep it affordable, use your current phone or, again, look for discounted ones on eBay* and Craigslist.

Chapter 17: Look good (affordably)

A lot of people assume that you can't dress nicely if you want to live frugally. It's absolutely not true.

Sure, retail clothes and beauty items can get pricey. But there are plenty of ways to avoid retail without sacrificing style.

Clothes

Shopping doesn't have to cost a bundle. Affordable options exist, even if you're not that into thrift stores.

Thrift stores – non-profits that sell donated items – do sometimes have some cool fashion finds. More often, you're just wading through things that people ditched for very good reasons.

Secondhand stores like Plato's Closet or Buffalo Exchange are a good alternative. These companies buy items from the public, so they're pickier about what they accept. In other words, you're more likely to find clothes you'd actually wear.

Finally, you have consignment stores. People bring in clothes (or furniture, toys, etc.) and have the store display and sell the items for them. The company takes a cut of the profits. For that reason, consignment prices tend to be a little higher than secondhand stores. Still, they're good for finding nice office attire or higher-end labels. They can also be great for finding fashionable maternity clothes.

Frugal tip: Be sure to bring any castoffs from your own closet to consignment or secondhand stores. If any are accepted, they'll offset the cost of the "new" stuff you buy.

If you prefer to buy truly new, try stores like TJ Maxx, Marshall's and Ross. These have great prices on some well-known brands. Last year I got a nice pair of Michael Kors dress pants for $40, and I've gotten some nice Max Azria/BCBG items there too.

Makeup

Makeup can be expensive. Still, some of us keep buying the overpriced stuff (I'm guilty of it) because we love very specific shades. We're convinced that we can't find the color at an affordable price.

Luckily, there are entire websites and Pinterest boards set up to find makeup "dupes" – that is, duplicates of the pricey stuff. If you're in love with an expensive product, check out Dupe That, Dupe Up and Temptalia's Makeup Dupe List to find that item's twin.

The sites show the products applied side-by-side on someone's skin, so you'll get a real idea of any differences. From what I've seen, they're practically identical. Any small variations are pretty much always worth the huge savings.

Hair products

Some people swear that the affordably priced stuff is just as good at the products you find in a salon. This is actually where I part ways with popular frugal opinion.

I've tried lesser brands, and I haven't been impressed with the results. Instead I use the admittedly overpriced products from

Bumble and Bumble.* To help make it more affordable, I ask for Sephora* gift cards for Christmas and birthdays.

If you're willing to explore more reasonably priced brands, I'd suggest checking out a beauty product review site like Makeup Alley. It has quite literally millions of reviews for more than 150,000 products, including makeup, hair, nails, grooming and skincare. Just plug in the name of the product you're curious about, and you can read in-depth assessments by site users.

If you don't have a specific product in mind, just Google "best affordable [product type] for [your hair type]." You'll find myriad posts listing the top contenders. I suggest reading at least three articles. The products mentioned on more than one site will be a good place to start.

You can use the same method to find skincare products. I don't have any useful suggestions. Nothing I use seems to change the dark circles under my eyes or my combination skin. On the other hand, that could be proof that drugstore brands are just as good (or bad) as department store ones.

Chapter 18: Frugal decorating

Stay away from Pinterest. I repeat: Stay away from Pinterest.

This could just be a personal quirk, but the site fills me with dread. It's a repository of things to feel bad about not being able to do: crafts, cooking, cleaning, decoration, organization and more.

There's an old curmudgeon in me that thinks, "Back in *my* day, we didn't have virtual boards to pin guilt-generating ideas to. We had to read magazines and have annoyingly efficient friends in order to find out all the things we should feel bad about not doing."

But seriously, this world is filled with ideas of ways to make your house look great cheaply and "easily." However, I rarely find the ideas all that easy.

Then again, the only walls with any color in our house are the ones in the living and dining rooms. I painted those and the kitchen cupboards when we moved in five years ago. Then I took a break and decided to do the rest later. I'm sure at least one more room will get painted before we pay off the mortgage. Probably.

In other words, I'm not going to suggest decorating that comes with a lot of effort. Hopefully, these will help you find a way to personalize your space without sacrificing your budget (or sanity).

Wall art

If you're in a college town, go to the student district for decorative pictures and posters. Failing that, sites like Art.com* and OnlinePosters.com* have a good selection and a lot of sales.

Once you have pictures and/or posters, get frames at Joann Fabrics* or Michael's* with one of their weekly coupons. Their coupons in the Sunday newspaper are also available on their websites. Each store takes its competitors' coupons, so be sure to check both to find the best offer.

You can also find nice frames for smaller pictures at Ross, TJMaxx, Marshall's, Tuesday Morning and even the dollar store. Some people find great frames at thrift shops, except that these may come with some ugly artwork attached. I suppose you can just donate the picture back to the store before you leave.

If you want something professionally framed, Joann Fabrics* regularly has discounts of up to 60% for the service. Just be sure not to get sucked into expensive bells and whistles. You don't need non-reflective glass or a ridiculously expensive mat. Be careful when pricing the frames, too. Some are pretty reasonable but others will be shockingly high for a craft store.

Of course, you don't always have to go for actual images. When I was really broke, I lived in an apartment with ugly cupboards. I absolutely hated the faux woodgrain.

Since I couldn't afford any nice art, I typed up quotes from some of my favorite books and taped them to the cupboard doors. Each morning when getting out my cereal bowl I'd see things like "If you worry about how you'll land, you'll never have a beautiful fall." To make things more visually interesting, you could always use old magazines to spell out the quotes ransom-note style.

Housewares

Trash cans, shower curtains, organizational baskets, decorative pillows and ornamental bowls are best found at Big Lots, TJ Maxx, Ross, Marshall's and Tuesday Morning. Big Lots tends to have the best prices on mirrors.

While all five stores offer bedsheets, I prefer to get my linens from Tuesday Morning. It probably has the nicest ornamental glassware too – which I might actually get if we didn't have a cat. The store also has very nice lamps, but even its discounted lamps are too rich for my blood. I prefer to get those at thrift stores, yard sales or Craigslist.

Dollar stores are great for vases (and decorative pebbles to put into those vases if that's your type of thing). Remember that vases can be used as much for storage as flowers; I use one to hold my hairbrushes. You can also get some baskets at dollar stores. These tend to be a bit on the flimsy side, but they're great for holding lighter items like keys, pill bottles and mail.

Bookcases are always expensive. If you have access to a truck, thrift stores and yard sales are the best way to go. Failing that, Best Buy* has full-size bookcases for about $50. They're not the highest quality, but they'll do the job.

One man's trash

If you live in an apartment complex, especially a community with multiple buildings, there's probably a discard pile somewhere on the premises. It's usually by the garbage bin, but not always. Find this area and check it regularly, especially towards the end of the month. As people get ready to move they suddenly realize some things aren't worth hauling.

At our former apartment complex this area was dubbed "the mall." We got a small bookcase and a TV stand, both of which we're still using six years later. My mom had some great finds at her own apartment building: a kitchen cart, some wooden chairs, a small bookcase and a portable shopping cart.

Another great place for discarded items: college and university districts. Students are either going back home for the summer or leaving for new cities after graduation. Either way, they generally don't want to pay to take bigger furniture items with them. Close to the end of the school year you can find everything from microwave ovens to big-screen televisions.

Chapter 19: Frugal gift-giving

Even healthy people find the holidays stressful. Figuring out what to get people (and how to make it fit in the budget) isn't for the faint of heart. So it can be exponentially more difficult for depressives to navigate gift-giving. Luckily, there are some great strategies to reduce the cost and tension.

Limit gifts

The best thing might be not to exchange presents at all. Float the idea to friends and/or family and see how it goes over.

This might be tough to do, since it can feel like a form of confrontation. But you'd be surprised how many people would be relieved at the thought of taking a name off their list. Propose instead that you just spend some time together in December – maybe getting a drink to complain about holiday stress.

Tip: Invite the person/people to your place, if you're up to hosting. Make it a BYOB and provide mixers and snacks. It's cheaper than going out for drinks *and* a lot of people abandon their leftover booze. Free alcohol!

If you meet with resistance, you can always play the depressive card. It's okay to remind people that you are, in fact, sick. They wouldn't expect someone with double pneumonia to put on the perfect holiday, right? All you're asking for is the same consideration.

Tell them that gift-giving is stressful and not good for your mental health (or your budget). Understanding friends and family will probably concede your point. As for people who don't... maybe they shouldn't be on your list (gift or social) anyway.

If you don't want to propose that radical of an idea – or if you just want to make sure *you* get a present – then suggest a name exchange. That way each person has to buy only one gift, which cuts down significantly on the stress of buying. Bonus: You don't have to worry about getting an unexpected present from someone you didn't buy for.

Shop online

You don't have to brave the crowds at the mall to be a good gift-giver. Even Black Friday sales are now mainly online, with the exception of perhaps a few ultra, mega, never-to-be-repeated-in-this-lifetime (until next year) doorbusters.

Since I personally don't need a new laptop or TV, I'm happy to stay at home. I suggest you do the same. While other people are standing in long lines, you'll be sitting comfortably in front of the computer and taking care of your gift list with a few clicks.

Be sure to sign up for Black Friday ad sites like BFads or the BradsDeals Black Friday website. These will keep you up to date on leaked ads, which will help you compare prices ahead of time. That way, all you have to do on Thanksgiving is enjoy turkey and keep your mouse-clicking hand warmed up.

Shopping online also means the potential for rebates. As I've said before, most major retailers are on cash back sites, so you can combine ridiculous deals with cash back bonuses. It's a match made in frugality heaven!

To recap: The benefits of shopping online are shopping in your PJs (or less – it's the holidays, go crazy) while eating leftover pumpkin pie, easily finding deals and getting cash back. The downside to shopping online is that you miss out on getting trampled for a TV.

Gift cards

This one is controversial. Some people think that gift cards are impersonal, i.e., that you're putting no effort into the present.

I disagree. Gift cards can show that you know the person and put thought into the purchase. In fact, they tell recipients that you know the stores they love (and that they're the best people to pick items in those stores).

It's even better if you can choose a GC to places the recipients don't normally indulge in due to price. I'm not talking about a $25 gift card for Ruth's Chris, but a how about GC for a high-end makeup brand, nice chocolates or a massage? Now *that's* a thoughtful gift.

If you want to sponsor an indulgence but don't want to dictate the exact use, pick up a gift card for an aggregate company. For example, SpaFinder* works with a lot of different stores that offer spa treatments (from pedicures to facials to massages).

This lets the recipient choose exactly how to use it. Meanwhile, you still get to make sure the money goes toward pampering rather than Pampers, A Walgreens* or Amazon* GC might be used for family items.

Don't forget to check out the discount gift card sites for your purchases. You can save a few bucks, and the card comes right to your door!

Set price limits

I almost hesitate to mention this one, since I see a lot of potential for it backfiring. After all, it's hard enough to find the perfect gift for someone. Trying to find the perfect gift *and* keeping it under $25 may prove maddening in a very literal sense.

On the other hand, a price limit could assuage depressives' often increased levels of guilt and anxiety. Knowing that there's a spending cap keeps you from worrying that you'll give some decorative candles and receive a $200 purse. With a price limit, you never have to worry about whether you're spending "enough" on someone.

As with so many frugal hacks, this is one that is based entirely on your judgment. Some people will find that the spending restriction alleviates more stress than it causes. Others will have the opposite experience. Be realistic, and approach this one with caution.

Chapter 20: Save your savings

Great, you've adopted some wonderful frugal habits and are saving a bunch of money. So... where is it?

Did that money go into your savings account? Get applied to a student loan or consumer debt? Or did it just vanish into the ether of general spending?

Maybe you're one of those people who barely makes ends meet, who needs to use all available funds just to cover basic expenses. In that case, it's understandable if you can't point to the money. Otherwise you need to corral those savings.

I created a Saved Savings account. Each time we save money with a frugal hack or other money-smart choice, I transfer that amount into Saved Savings.

Getting rid of Dish Network* saved us $92 a month; switching to Ooma gave us another $30 a month; our Internet bill went down $10. Pretty much any time we save money – including cash back rebates – I try to put the savings into the Saved Savings account. At the end of each month I dump the balance into the main savings account and start all over again.

Since depressives are so prone to negative thinking, we need to do everything we can to boost morale – and concrete evidence of progress is a great motivator. Watching the account balance grow helps keep us on task. The savings are *tangible* – or as tangible as money can be in the digital age.

Chapter 21: What you *should* spend on

There are a few things which you should never skimp on. This doesn't mean you should lavish money on these areas. What it *does* mean is that you shouldn't automatically go for the cheapest option.

Mental health

If you can't cope, you can't save money – or do much of anything. Your first priority is to keeping yourself healthy. At the very least this means finding money in the budget for therapy and any medications.

Can't afford therapy? Therapy on a sliding scale probably exists in your region; do an online search for "sliding scale therapy [your city]."

You'll have more options if you live in or near a college town. Post-graduate students in psychology and social work need a certain number of supervised hours with patients before they can begin working on their own. This is often done through a sliding scale therapy program.

These programs will work with you based on the state of your finances. I've paid anywhere from $5 to $30 per session.

If you can't afford your mental health medication, check out sites like RxAssist and Partnership for Prescription Assistance. These will help you find programs that may pay some or all of the cost. The PPA site will also help you find free or low-cost clinics near you.

But mental health isn't all about Western medicine. Some depressives find activities like yoga, meditation and even gardening to be immensely therapeutic. If that's the case with you, try to find room in the budget for them.

That said, don't get carried away when you're just starting out. Try one or two yoga sessions (no matter how appealing that 10-class discount is) to see if it's right for you. Or check YouTube for yoga videos. Just choose the channel carefully. Be sure the person is a yoga instructor, not just a yoga enthusiast, or you may end up hurting yourself.

Look for free digital downloads for guided meditation. If it seems promising, then go looking on iTunes.

Buy seeds at the dollar store (where they cost as little as a quarter), and look for a cheap trowel, too; if you can't find gardening tools there, buy the lower-end ones at the department or hardware store.

The point is that you can always upgrade later. While you're just getting started, you don't want to throw a lot of money toward something that might not pan out. Doing so could cause guilt and regret – which are things depressives certainly don't need more of.

Rent

I've got nothing against a cheap place to live, but sometimes these places are cheap for a reason. Living in a dank little hole or an apartment riddled with roaches may exacerbate your depression. You might find that you'll spend more time away from the apartment – which can get expensive – simply because you can't handle the idea of going home to such an unpleasant environment.

Find a place that you think you can actually be comfortable in. It doesn't have to (and shouldn't) be a penthouse but it doesn't have to be in the basement. A unit that gets at least a little sunlight is probably best.

Don't go too far out of the town for cheap rent either. Sure, rents get lower the further you go from popular areas, but you shouldn't isolate yourself. It's also important to choose a place close to a drugstore and supermarket, so it's as easy as possible to get your medications and food.

None of this is a license to pay sky-high rent. But please make sure you're not overzealous about getting the cheapest living space.

Furniture

You need a good bed. Depression worsens when you're tired, so a good night's sleep is essential. Pay a little more to get a mattress that ensures restful. If you can't afford a good bed, check Amazon* for affordable mattress toppers to make your current bed more comfortable.

You also need an incredibly comfortable chair or couch, so you'll feel cozy while you watch TV or read. This is also a good place to curl up when you're having a bad day.

In the past I've gotten some wonderful couches at thrift stores, but nowadays the threat of bedbugs looms large. You *probably* won't get an infested chair or couch, but if you do, you'll have to replace everything, including your bed. That's why I shy away from buying upholstered furniture secondhand.

Besides, getting larger items home is an issue. Thrift shops rarely deliver and most cars can't fit a big chair, let alone a couch.

You'll need to have either a truck or a very obliging, truck-owning friend. It's possible to rent a vehicle, but then you'd have a very finite window to find the right furniture.

It's probably best to shop retail if you can afford it. First, haunt the clearance sections of furniture stores, especially chains. My husband and I went couch-shopping when Mor Furniture was taking an extra 50% off clearance items. Our leather couch cost us around $350 after taxes, *and* we got free delivery.

If you don't have good luck with clearance, then know your holiday furniture sales. Presidents Day and Labor Day weekend tend to have some pretty good prices. The fact that they're weekend sales gives you a better chance to make it to the store before the deals end.

Not up to leaving the house? There are plenty of sites known for discounted furniture and cheap shipping. You'll pay $2.95 to ship Overstock.com* orders of $40 or less; larger ones ship free. SmartBargains* has free shipping on any order.

Haircut

Your head is (probably) the first thing people see when they meet you. There's no hiding a bad haircut. So unless your hair is all one length *and* you have an incredibly steady and precise hand, don't act as your own stylist. Don't even trust your friend who swears she can *totally* cut your hair.

I've been lucky to find some good beauty schools that give great service for a fraction of the retail salon cost. (Currently I pay $30 for a cut and color.) However, not everyone is comfortable taking that leap. In that case you'll need to find a salon you trust to give good quality. If it's a chain like Regis, use discounted GCs to help temper the cost.

Wherever you go, bring a picture for any new style you want to try. Print out cute cuts from the Internet or browse the salon's hair magazines until you find the right look. Because if a picture is worth a thousand words, then it's worth a *million* vaguely stated descriptions like "Well, you know, a little bit shorter. I mean not *too* short, but… shorter. And I think it's layered a little on the sides, but maybe not."

Shoes

No Manolo Blahniks, of course. But quality shoes are important. You need something with good support and cushioning. These may not be cheap, but neither is a podiatrist.

It's also best to have more than one pair to use regularly. Footwear needs a day to properly dry out; if it doesn't, then bacteria can form and the shoe material will break down faster. Have at least two pairs of shoes and wear them on alternate days. Your footwear will last significantly longer overall.

Also, I beg you: Don't buy used shoes. People tread differently, which causes shoes to get worn in very specific ways. Your own walking patterns may be very different. If so, used shoes can cause pain and even make you risk rolling your ankle.

There are a lot of places to get shoes for less than retail: Shoebuy,* Famous Footwear,* Payless Shoe Source,* OnlineShoes.com,* Kohl's*/Macy's*/jcpenney*/Sears* sales, outlet malls and more. So just buy new.

Socializing

Getting out is one of the hardest parts of depression. You need to take advantage of opportunities to leave the house. Isolation, while technically frugal, can exacerbate bad spells, which may make you fall off the wagon in other areas of spending.

Happy hours are your friend. As I suggested in the Comfort Spending section, Google "best happy hours [your city]" to get an idea of the best deals and which days of the week to find them. Keep a list, in case a friend suddenly proposes an evening out. You'll be able to make informed suggestions and save both of you some money. Just remember to order exclusively from the discounted drinks and food menu.

If happy hour is over, then order well drinks. Lower-end brands of alcohol pack the same punch as the pricey stuff. Besides, it's all getting mixed into juice or soda, so what does it matter?

Alternatively, you could just be the designated driver. Your friends will probably spring for your soda – cheaper than a taxi, after all – and some bars even offer free soda to the DD. Otherwise, get some water and make an excuse for not drinking. If you take antidepressants, you can truthfully say that you're not supposed to have alcohol with the medication you're on.

Of course, there's nothing saying that socializing has to be done at a retail establishment. Have friends over or go to a friend's house. Watch a movie, chat, or, if there are enough of you, have a game night.

Chapter 22: So you think you can frugal

Maybe you feel like you've got a handle on the basics of saving money. (Or maybe you've at least run through the basics, no matter what the outcome.) If so, you may feel ready for an intermediate course in frugality. Check out these budget-friendly tactics:

Calling for discounts

Periodically contact your Internet provider, cable provider (if you decide not to cut the cord) and any other companies you subscribe to and see if there are any discounts they can provide. If you get an offer in the mail from another company, reference that. Or just use the "I've been a good customer for X years now…" approach.

Every year or two you should look for a better deal on auto insurance. The personal finance site NerdWallet has a rate comparison tool that doesn't require you to give a phone number.

Skip the dryer

Fabrics take quite a beating in the dryer. Save yourself quarters, keep your electricity bill lower and make your items last longer by using drying racks.

You might luck out and find these in thrift stores or at yard sales. If not, racks are pretty affordable at stores like Target* and Walmart.* Use discounted gift cards to make them even cheaper.

Some things you'll still want to throw in the dryer, like sheets and comforters. But the rest of your laundry will fit pretty easily on a couple of drying racks. Shirts can be hung to dry on plastic hangers.

Cash challenges

The most common of these is probably the dollar-bill challenge. Every night you take all $1 bills from your wallet and put them in a jar. The results are apparently astonishing. I'll have to take that on faith since I rarely use cash.

If a dollar at a time is too rich for your blood, choose quarters or even pennies. Small amounts add up faster than you think. My husband, who uses cash more often than I do, empties his wallet of all change when he gets home. Quarters go in one jar, dimes and nickels into another. Pennies go into an actual bank.

Originally he separated his coins for easy access in case of ice cream trucks. (When you live next to a park, you'll eventually cave.) But it's evolved into a good way to save our change, even when tinny music isn't playing.

Another option – the one easiest for virtual bankers like myself – is the weekly challenge. The first week, you put $1 into a separate account. The second week, you put in $2. And so on and so forth as long as your budget can manage it. I'm in the middle of this challenge right now. Given our set weekly limit, I won't be able to make it too far into the year. Still, if I can get up to even the 20th week, that'll be $210 saved!

Reuse/repair

Not to encourage a frugal stereotype, but…The cost of Ziploc bags *does* add up. Consider rinsing them out quickly, turning them inside out and letting them dry overnight.

Some grocery stores give a cash credit for each shopping bag you bring. (Only the ones that you use, of course. Don't come in with a garbage bag's worth, expecting a payday.) Keep a bunch in your car so that you never have to worry about forgetting them.

Get a few extra dish towels at the dollar store rather than constantly buying and tossing paper towels. (Bonus: It's one less thing to run out of.)

When something breaks, see if you can get it fixed. We took our vacuum cleaner to a repair shop. For under $18 we got a working appliance rather than pay $80 to $120 for a new one.

Busted shoe? There are still cobblers around. According to Business Insider, a $20 to $50 fix can give your kicks an extra few years of use.

When something goes awry in your home, do a quick Internet troubleshoot before you call a professional. While I'm not suggesting you become Mr. or Ms. Fixit, you might find that a real repair isn't needed. For example, suppose your garbage disposal stops in mid-grind. Very often it's a simple question of pushing the reset button.

And if something isn't fixable? See if you can sell it. There are lots of listings on eBay for broken gadgetry, and someone on Craigslist may give you $5 to $10 for a broken table or a sofa with a bad leg. If it's something you don't want to have to haul away, put it in the free section of Craigslist or advertise it on Freecycle. Handy folks out there may actually want it.

Reusing items boosts your budget and also reduces your carbon footprint on Earth. But if it's not always possible, don't beat yourself up about it.

Free movies

Advance screenings are a great way to see films absolutely free. You get screening passes that let you (plus one) in to a theater where you can see a movie before it even comes out.

Websites like Wild About Movies, AdvanceScreenings.com and gofobo let you know about screenings in U.S. and Canadian cities. You have to jump on these pretty quickly, so be sure to check your e-mail regularly. Or use Twitter: Follow the sites Advance Screenings (@screenings) or Free Movie Screening (@screeningticket).

Another source of passes is the newspaper, specifically the alternative weeklies. (Bonus: The alt weeklies are usually free.) Or listen for giveaways at radio stations, which get preview tickets from movie studios anxious to generate buzz.

Sometimes you have to send away for them. This was a big barrier for me, as I hate dealing with mail. Or you have to go to a certain store to pick up the passes, which usually means going up to the cashier and asking for a ticket. That always felt a little awkward, since I clearly wasn't buying anything; but no employee ever seemed to care.

Luckily, my Mom was always happy to do that stuff for me. Ask any cinephile friends or family members if they'd be willing to do the same. Make them a deal: You find the offers, they get the pass, and you both enjoy the movie.

Once you have your pass, make sure you get there early. Screenings are intentionally overbooked. Unfortunately, this means that, even in a best-case scenario, you'll probably stand/sit in line for an hour or so before getting in.

Be sure to take advantage of the "plus one" on the pass. Besides good company, there'll be someone to hold your spot if you have to use the bathroom. If you do fly solo it's best to bring something to do and/or headphones. Otherwise you may get sucked into social interaction.

This hack definitely have some potential trip-ups. Still, it costs almost nothing (other than stamps or gas/bus fare) to try. Meanwhile, you'll get to see free movies – before all the paying customers!

Local attractions

Many museums have one or more free days per month. You won't be able to see any special exhibits, but you'll be able to go and look at the history/art/dinosaur bones as long as your little eyes can bear it. (Or until closing time.)

If you miss the free day, you've still got options:

The Museums On Us program involves 150 museums in 31 states. You just need a Bank of America bank account or a credit/debit card from BofA or Merrill Lynch. Any of those will get you in for free on the first Saturday of the month (plus some Sundays).

Incidentally, you don't have to be into fine art to enjoy this benefit. A few interesting places on the list are the Motown Museum, the IGFA Fishing Hall of Fame, the National Cowboy

& Western Heritage Museum, the Shedd Aquarium, the Houston Zoo and the Country Music Hall of Fame.

Already a museum member? Get more bang for your membership buck with museum reciprocity.

The North American Reciprocal Museum Association has more than 800 participating institutions across the continent. That includes not just the U.S. and Canada, but also Bermuda, El Salvador and Mexico. Again, it's not all art. Check out cultural, historical, scientific and even children's museums, as well as botanical gardens.

There are more regional programs too. The Southeastern Reciprocal Membership program includes institutions in 12 U.S. states (as far north as Pennsylvania and as far west as Mississippi), Puerto Rico and the U.S. Virgin Islands. You'll have access to arts, crafts, design, history and science museums.

Want to get your nerd on? The Association of Science and Technology Centers has more than 600 member museums in nearly 50 countries. Its passport program provides free general admission to participating museums (with some local restrictions).

More than 220 museums belong to The Association of Zoos and Aquariums. Join one and get free or discounted admission to any that participate in the program.

The Association of Children's Museums network includes 200 museums. You need to have a premium family membership with network benefits, but that will give you half-off general admission for up to six people at a time.

You may also have local resources. As I mentioned earlier, Phoenix libraries have passes available for checkout.

Unfortunately, these passes have even shorter lending periods than library books, which is why I avoid them. Too much stress for me. Still, some people might find the deadline motivating. Having a due date might get them out of the house in time to enjoy the museum.

Rewards programs

Swagbucks is a rewards program with a ton of ways to earn points, including but not limited to watching videos, taking surveys and doing Internet searches. You cash in rewards for gift cards or PayPal payments. I usually go for Amazon GCs because it has most of the things we need to buy. With Swagbucks GCs, we've gotten collectibles, books, graphic novels, clothes, video games and consoles – and plenty of boring, adult things like shoes, toilet paper, razors and shampoo.

Swagbucks has saved us thousands of dollars over the years. I could write an entire chapter about this rewards program all on its own, but it's simpler to just direct you to my blog post, Swagbucks for Beginners. If you're interested, check that out. If you're not, then you don't have to flip through several pages wondering when I'll stop worshipping at the Swagbucks altar.

Another great rewards program is My Coke Rewards. Don't drink much soda? This might still work (more on that in a minute).

You may have noticed the codes on Coke products, under the cap or printed on multi-pack boxes. Plug these into the MCR website for points that you can cash in for e-gift cards (including Amazon) or for physical prizes.

My favorite category is the AMC movie packages. There's an option for one ticket plus a fountain drink, but I prefer the next level up: two gold tickets (aka any show any time, even when it's just been released), two large drinks and a large popcorn.

Even if you don't drink much soda (or Minute Maid juices or Dasani flavored waters), you can ask friends and family to save them for you. Or get even more creative: My mom's been known to snatch empty bottles from the tops of trash cans, and to pull multipack boxes out of the mixed-paper bin at the recycling center.

In short, My Coke Rewards is an amazing program that allows us to see movies – and get pricey concessions – without paying a dime.

Rewards programs like MyPoints and Inbox Dollars operate by sending emails that you can click on for points (MyPoints) and cash (Inbox Dollars).

However, the earnings are somewhat slow to accrue – unless you opt for big-ticket actions like online shopping and free-trial offers. You'll get much better deals online shopping through cash back sites. And free trials... Well, I have more to say about that later in the book.

Batch cooking

Batch cooking is simply making a lot of food(s) and putting much of it in the freezer. It's similar to Erin Chase's program, except that these meals are already cooked. You can thaw them overnight or microwave them back to non-Ice-Age temperatures.

Knowing that there are several meal options at home is a great way to talk yourself out of convenience food's sodium-filled siren song. It also means less stress during a bad spell, when you can't face anything more challenging than a microwave.

One-pot-glop meals are ideal for batch cooking, but the tactic works with any recipe that freezes well. If you have more than one slow cooker everything can be made simultaneously for extra ease.

Just take the normal recipes and double (or even triple) the ingredients. Divide them among containers, write the name of the dish written on a strip of masking tape (most foods look alike in cryostasis) and put them on ice.

Don't overfill the containers, especially if you're only cooking for one or two people. Otherwise you run the risk of leftovers fatigue, which opens the door to rationalizing convenience food. Having at least two different meals in the fridge at any given time gives some semblance of variety.

Rewards cards

A lot of rewards credit cards will waive their fee for the first year, and provide generous sign-up bonuses.

The idea is to close the account before you're charged the next year's fee, then move on to the next rewards card bonus. "Credit card churning" is a great frugal hack – but only if you're good with deadlines. As previously noted, due dates can be a real problem for depressives.

Otherwise, go for a rewards card without an annual fee. You usually won't get a sign-up bonus but at least you'll get rewarded for the money you spend. The best one I've heard about so far is the Citi Double Cash Back card. You'll get 1% when you charge something and another 1% when you pay it off.

And you're *always* paying your bill in full, right? If not, you need to avoid credit cards as much as possible, but that's a subject for another book.

No-spend days

The name is probably obvious, but a no-spend day simply means a day where you don't buy anything. It can make you get more creative but at times could prove to be very stressful. If you decide to try this, plan ahead of time. Make sure you have enough gas in your car, that your bus pass isn't about to expire, that there's food in the fridge, and so on.

Alternately, you can pick a single type of spending for a no-spend week. Choose it very carefully, i.e., make it one you can realistically do. If you're prone to needing comfort food during bad spells, don't choose "takeout" or "junk food" as the cutback category.

Some people take this even further with no-spend *months*. I think that's far too extreme a goal for most people, let alone depressives.

Remember that there are no actual stakes in this, no repercussions if you don't succeed. It's a challenge. It's optional. No need for a shame spiral if you wind up buying some Red Vines during a no-candy week.

Mystery shopping

Mystery shopping is by far one of the best ways to enjoy life. I've gotten free drinks, food, movie tickets, rental cars, water park admission, arcade play and hotel stays. I even got paid to gamble!

It's an awesome way to go out without killing the budget. But there are a few catches.

- You have to visit within a certain time frame.
- You have to be sure you observe carefully and ask specific questions.
- You have to write up a report afterward – usually within two or three days of the trip.
- You have to foot the bill initially.

That last one might be the most intimidating, since it puts extra pressure on meeting the reporting deadline. That said, I've always gotten my reimbursement – and I did a *lot* of shops that required an initial outlay on my part.

Honestly, most of them are well worth the effort. The reports are generally pretty short. And it's even easier to take notes these days thanks to smartphones. (Back in the day I had to keep sneaking off to the bathroom to scribble notes.)

If you want to learn more, I recommend *The Ultimate Resource Guide*, which is written by a blogger who has been mystery shopping for more than 15 years. She provides a clear explanation of how to get started and the companies from which she has gotten the most benefit, along with information on other money-making hustles like panel studies and product testing.

You can also find a fair amount of free information on Volition.com. Free is always great, but if you want actual guidance in addition to information – and you probably do, even if you don't realize it – then I suggest spending the money for *The Ultimate Resource Guide*. Once you've done three mystery shops, you'll have more than recouped the cost.

Chapter 23: How to manage the hacks (and life in general)

You might be so excited by these ideas that you're already planning a coordinated attack on multiple financial fronts.

Please, please don't.

As I said at the beginning of this book, it's best to focus on just one – at most two – hacks at a time. You need to get each one down before moving on to the next challenge.

Even mentally healthy frugal people zero in on one or two money-saving tricks at a time. Sure, they're constantly looking to improve; but they know better than to try too much at once. That just leads to frugal burnout. Instead, they tackle one cost-saving tactic at a time until it's a habit. Then they move on to the next hack.

It might seem like everyone but you is constantly making the right money choices. Actually, they've just created routines and habits that pretty much run themselves. They're able to be frugal in so many areas because so much of it is automatic:

- Their morning (or even pre-bedtime) routine includes packing a lunch
- They've set up low-priced subscriptions whenever possible.
- They automatically stock up during the best sales.
- They've created strict limits for indulgences.
- They've installed electricity- and water-saving devices

And so on and so forth. In short, they've worn financial grooves into their lives, and they're able to follow those without too much thought.

Since you're just getting started, it's important to have a small focus. This is just as important in life as it is in frugality.

Break it down

Depression can make even simple tasks feel gargantuan. They threaten to suck up every available ounce of energy and mental wherewithal. In short, they loom.

I've gone through an entire day without being able to make a very necessary, very simple phone call. For reasons I can't adequately explain, the idea of talking on the phone felt onerous. No, more than onerous. It felt impossible.

We depressives tend to take an all-or-nothing view. We think that we should be able to do the same things as "normal" people. So either we can, or we can't. We rarely leave room for an in-between option.

When a task seems too big to deal with, analyze the situation and, if possible, break down the task into the smallest possible components. Doing this should help you realize you're capable of more than you thought.

For example, one of the things I hate most is finding a new doctor or specialist. You have to call insurance, get names, choose one, make an appointment and, perhaps worst of all, *go* there. The enormity of it all makes me want to avoid the phone completely.

So I break it down:

1. Get out my insurance card

2. Call insurance to get names
3. Checking doctor ratings online
4. Call for an appointment (or request one online)

I let myself tackle as little as one step per day. Knowing that I don't have to do it all at once is a huge stress reliever – so much so that I sometimes manage to do it all in one fell swoop. When this happens I congratulate myself. When it doesn't, I'm still on schedule.

Sometimes tasks are less about steps and more about time. But you can break that down too. Need to clean? Set a timer for 10 or 15 minutes. Do everything you can in that time. As soon as the alarm sounds, stop. Seriously. *Stop.*

It's easier to get down to a task when you know it'll be over soon. Once the time is up, you have a feeling of accomplishment – and maybe a Swiffered kitchen and unloaded dishwasher, too.

When all else fails, don't be afraid to bribe yourself. Go online to pay a bill, then settle in for your favorite reality TV show. Clean the bathroom sink, then enjoy a big bowl of ice cream.

It might make you feel guilty, like you're not really an adult. On the other hand, adults *invented* bribery. And whether or not you're a "real" adult, you'll still have a clean(er) kitchen floor.

The *two*-do list

I take breaking things down to a whole new level. I break down my to-do list. A lot.

Unless life is particularly chaotic – and two people with chronic illnesses do tend to have low-level chaos at any given time – I keep no more than two things on my list each day. During hectic spells, with too much to do in too little time, I still make it a point to stop at four items.

I've found through trial and so, *so* much error that an exhaustive list of errands is overwhelming. Even if I only target a couple of things on any given day, the rest hover in the back of my mind. It starts to feel like I can't possibly make a dent, let alone get all of them done, which means I'm less inclined to tackle anything at all.

That's why I write down or focus on just one or two tasks. Furthermore, I make the tasks very small: making a call, going to an appointment or even sending my husband to mail something.

This includes frugal tasks too. An online purchase counts as a chore. (During bad spells, I break it into two: comparing prices and placing the order.) Paying a bill – online, over the phone or by mail – counts as a chore. Hitting a sale *definitely* counts as one.

Sometimes I'm a little sheepish about how few things I can deal with on any given day. Most of the time, however, I'm just relieved that I have simple, attainable goals. Think about it: If you get even *one* task done, you're either halfway or completely done for the day!

That sense of accomplishment is soothing. Knowing that I'm making headway keeps me going. In fact, sometimes the feeling of the success empowers me to take on an extra chore.

The two-chore method also keeps the stakes low. Some days I'm not in a position to get *anything* done. If I have a million things on my list, failing to make a dent fills me with shame and guilt. Sometimes a little panic gets thrown in too since the list keeps growing.

Conversely, not managing to do even one of two tasks is not a huge deal. The chores will be waiting for me the next day but the low number feels non-threatening. To help keep myself in that frame of mind I start focusing on a task long before it's due. You see, I'm a big believer in giving myself a wide berth for deadlines.

Give yourself time

Depression and deadlines don't mix. A hard-and-fast timeline doesn't mesh with bad days. A ticking clock adds stress, which interferes with a depressive's ability to function.

Alas, the world is full of due dates. There's no getting around them: At some point, you'll have to pay a bill, cancel a subscription, do your taxes, etc. And missing a due date has decidedly un-frugal results.

You might pay a late fee. You might have to keep paying for a service you don't want or no longer use. You could end up owing interest on overdue taxes.

We know all of these things, yet many of us fail to plan around our depression. Once again, it's a case of all or nothing. Maybe we're trying to prove to ourselves that we're fine. Perhaps we're just too ashamed to cut ourselves the slack we need.

Regardless of the reason, the result is the same: We're so desperate to prove that we're normal that we succumb to or exacerbate the symptoms of our illness. We can't bring ourselves to plan for reality, so instead we base our schedules on what we wish we were capable of.

When we fail to create realistic plans, we set ourselves up for disaster. We realize we can't manage it and start the slide down the shame spiral. Or we get it done, but our success is only by dint of the kind of manic, skin-of-our-teeth work that comes with a panicked last-minute efforts.

In other words, we end up with distressing failure or exhausting successes – both of which leave us emotionally and/or physically depleted in the face of the next deadline.

I lived that way for ages, but finally I couldn't take it anymore. So I did something radical: I started planning for reality. Nowadays, I give myself multiple reminders leading up to the actual deadline.

You see, I rarely do something the first time around. The first mention of it simply starts me thinking about the task. The second note either propels me to do it or at least sets the chore as a priority.

I pretty much always get it done before the third reminder; however, sometimes other categories of my life implode simultaneously. So I put a fourth note on the calendar for really important stuff, just in case.

No matter how many reminders I give myself, the last one will always be at least one day before the actual deadline. This method has worked for several tasks thus far, from getting ready to appear on podcasts to more serious matters such as mailing insurance premiums.

Nowhere is that more evident than the December page in our 2016 calendar.

We're using a rewards credit card to finance a trip this fall. There was a great signup bonus, but there was also a hefty annual fee starting in 2017. And there's no way in hell I'm paying $95 for the privilege of using a card.

So my calendar has the following:

December 1st: Cancel credit card

December 10th: Cancel card

December 18th: Cancel credit card

December 29th: Seriously, cancel the damn card!

(Given the stakes in this case, that last reminder is still about two weeks before the cancel date. I'm not taking any chances.)

You probably think this is funny. Or maybe you find it sad. I find it helpful. And frankly I think a lot of depressives would benefit from this system.

As I keep mentioning, stress is our downfall. The more stressed we are, the harder it is to function – even when that involves tackling and thereby eliminating the stressor. By giving yourself time to work up to a task, you're making the task more manageable. The more manageable something is, the less stress accompanies it.

If there's a great sale, plan to go on the first day. This gives you a little leeway to, once again, build up to it. I recommend avoiding one-day sales whenever possible. If you're having a good day, then great, take advantage; personally, I find they cause more stress and frustration than anything.

Giving yourself time when you have none

Obviously, some things are more time sensitive than others. You might not have long between payday and a bill's due date. In that case, plan ahead. Take the time beforehand to write out the check (if you still do such things), put it in an envelope and slap a stamp on it. That way, you can drop it in the mail as soon as you know the funds are in your account.

If you pay bills electronically, you may be able to designate what day the funds will be withdrawn. It's best to allow a one- or two-day window between the deposit and payment, just in case.

Can't schedule a payment ahead of time? Then be sure to mark up your digital and/or paper calendar to keep yourself on the ball. Seeing a reminder that *isn't* last-minute may help defuse the stress of the deadline.

And sometimes you just have to make your peace with late fees. I'm not advocating a lax attitude toward due dates, but at times you may have fewer coping skills than you do deadlines. Something has to give – and you need to make sure it's not your sanity.

In the end, it's about triage. Figure out what absolutely can't fall by the wayside, and then do your best with what's left.

Your credit card should be one of the first things you take care of. It's not just the nasty $35 late fee, but also the interest charges and the possibility of having your card issuer jack up your interest rate. Credit card due dates are the worst ones to miss, whereas other bills may have little to no late fees as long as you pay within a few days.

If you do make a late payment on a credit card, most banks will waive the fee as a courtesy once a year. You'll be stuck with the interest charges though, so keep those card balances low!

Trying trials

I like to say that I work best on a deadline. What I actually mean is that I can't make myself get things done without the rush of dread and adrenaline that comes with last-minute pressure.

Most of the time that propels me into action, though it leaves me too drained to handle the next time-sensitive item. Well, at least until I'm staring down *that* deadline. Still, it keeps me going... usually.

Unfortunately, sometimes a due date creates so much dread that I'm paralyzed. Just thinking about the deadline makes my soul shrivel, and all I want to do is... anything else, really. But realistically, it probably involves binge-watching something or hiding under the covers. Or both.

Weirdly, errands with the lowest stakes tend to create the most dread. (Maybe they just don't generate enough adrenaline.) My worst track record has always been cancelling subscriptions and membership.

I've gotten stuck in plenty of unwanted, unused services because I was trying to be frugal. You see, I love rewards programs and one of the quickest ways to get rewards is to sign up for a free trial. After all, there's no obligation. You can cancel at any time!

That always sounded great, right up until the deadline drew near. Then I'd start to picture calling the company and dealing with a customer service representative who'd try to talk me into staying. Sometimes, I'd simply feel sheepish about rejecting the representative's company. (Did I mention my depression comes with a side of overactive guilt?)

In the end, I'd be unable to face the interaction, thus dooming myself to a few months' of service simply because I couldn't make a phone call. At one point in my mid-20s, I ended up with about six months' worth of diet supplements because I couldn't just call and cancel. I still had four of the bottles when I moved almost a year later.

And let's not even get into my misadventures with Columbia House.

The point is, I so wanted to be the kind of person who *could* deal with deadlines that I'd convince myself I was. It was putting undue strain on my already fragile emotional state – and my bank account.

Eventually I wised up. Clearly, "free" was costing me too much. I stopped signing up, and my life got a lot easier.

(Back and forth) over the line

By and large, I've found it easier (and healthier) for me to draw a line in the sand. On one side there are the things I can do and on the other, things I can't. Mostly I try to be at peace with the latter and find ways to optimize the rest.

This has helped me immensely. Accepting that there are things I simply can't do has virtually stopped my slides down the shame spiral.

Yet there's a part of me that still bristles at "can't," the part that believes that setting unilateral limits isn't good for my self-esteem. It makes me feel as though I'm not as good as a healthy person – even though, in reality, it's just that I'm less well than one.

It's important to remember is that depression makes life harder, not impossible. The same goes for the head-to-head match of depression and frugality. So from time to time I take a deep breath and try again – but with a few safeguards in place.

First I analyze what went wrong before: Where was the failure in the system? Next I ask myself how I can guard against that in the future. Sometimes, the answer is that I can't. If it isn't possible to find a way to work around my depressive limitations, then I abandon the idea as not worth my time and limited energy.

Happily, there are times that I *can* come up with a new plan of attack. That could be something as simple as asking Tim to help. While he's also a depressive, he'll do everything in his power to make my life easier.

But there's a crucial component for the new attempt: forgiveness. I remind myself that my previous efforts failed, and I think about what would happen if I'm not successful a second time. Can I handle that or will it send me under the covers, wailing with guilt?

Sometimes it's not worth the risk. Other times, I decide that it'll be okay, that failure *is* an option. In that case, I try again – at least twice. If the first attempt doesn't work, I re-analyze the issue again to see if there are any other options. Then I try once more.

If I still don't succeed, I scoot the task back over the line to "can't," albeit with an option to try again at some future date. Or maybe it'll stay over that line forever. What's important is that I'm not giving up on myself, but I'm also not risking my mental health trying to prove something.

Chapter 24: Depression symptoms (and how to frugal around them)

Okay, we've discussed how to adapt frugal hacks around your depression. Now it's time to look at how to stay frugal during particularly bad spells.

Anti-social tendencies

Depression can make social interaction difficult. You either can't bear to deal with people or can't bear the people you have to deal with. If it's tough to get yourself to make phone calls or trips to the store, you'll probably wind up paying premiums (or late fees) to avoid leaving the house.

Fortunately, the digital age has made misanthropy a little more affordable.

If you dread the post office, you can pay and print the postage online, then drop the package on the post-office counter and leave. (Bonus: Paying online usually comes with a discount.) Or take it a step further and schedule a pick-up. The postal worker will come to your door for the package, and you can even get Priority Mail boxes delivered to your home.

Shopping online for most items means you can avoid the stores. You may even find better prices, especially if you're using online coupons and/or cash back sites. This isn't just for household items, either. Pizzerias often have online-only deals. Other restaurants let you order online and then swing by to collect your order; some will actually bring the food out to the curb for pickup.

You can even order groceries online. Supermarkets charge a small fee but it might be worth the money to avoid the hassle, especially if you don't normally use physical coupons. Specialty options like Amazon PrimePantry and PeaPod* also bring groceries to your door.

Online food shopping has a great secondary benefit: fewer impulse purchases! Since you're not roaming the aisles, you won't see all the displays designed to make you add items to your cart. You won't be tempted by the aroma of freshly baked cookies or French bread.

Apathy

Sometimes you just can't bring yourself to care. Depression often causes exhaustion. When you're already weary, the work involved in saving money might not seem worth it. At other times depression deadens your emotions. Saving money might no longer hold meaning for you, so why force yourself to put in the effort?

Well, because Future You will care. And no offense, but Future You is probably kind of bitchy.

Scriously, think how hard you are on yourself already. Do you think Future You is going to be any nicer? No, Future You is probably going to Monday-morning-quarterback the hell of the decisions you're making now.

So if you can't care right now, care about not being judged later – especially by your own worst critic. Each time you plumb the depths and come up with "I don't care," ask yourself how much guilt that'll cause later. Hopefully, it'll be enough to motivate you.

Of course, it helps if you make things easier to deal with.

One reader who struggles with apathy said that having a banking app helps. During the worst spells, it's simply too much work to go over to the computer, turn it on and log in to her bank account. However, she *can* make herself double tap an icon on her phone.

This a great example of structuring your life realistically – which involves taking some time on good days to find workarounds for the bad ones.

Too apathetic to make food? If you're normally able to cook, be sure always to have leftovers around, even if they're in the freezer. Microwaves can thaw things pretty quickly. Or keep a stash of convenience food in the house. If neither of those tactics work, be sure your budget includes a "takeout and delivery" category.

Can't make yourself to leave the house for a sale? Stock up on good days and you won't have to worry about it. Or aim to go on the first day of the sale, which gives you a little leeway to build up to it. With luck, the bad spell will be over before the sale is.

Stressed about saving? Automate $20 a week, $50 per paycheck or whatever works for you. Bonus: Watching the numbers grow from month to month will help you feel more financially secure.

And what if none of these tactics work? What if you're still ignoring account alerts, ordering in and buying toilet paper at the convenience store?

Well, maybe that's okay… occasionally.

Depression is a disease. Some days are going to be bad. That's just the way it is. We can waste our time and energy feeling guilty about it, or we can allow ourselves the rest that our bodies and/or brains apparently need.

On a day when it's clear nothing will get done, at least *try* to relax into it and accept it. Hopefully you'll come out of the experience recharged, which can help alleviate the guilt of an unproductive day. (Arguably, though, taking care of yourself is one of the best things you can do. So you *did* get something done!)

Focus

Concentration is one of the first things to go during my depressive spells. Well, unless the topic is what a bad person I am. My brain is totally on board for that one.

Normally I can focus when it's quiet. During bad depression spells, however, I used to need a second stimulus to keep me focused on the main one. In college I had to play music while studying or my mind would wander away from the class notes. At one point it was so bad that I had to read a book during class lectures in order to focus on what the professor was saying.

These days I need quiet in order to focus. I have a hard time concentrating when something is going on in the background. I find that complete quiet is almost never possible, so I've adapted with a white noise app and noise cancelling ear buds.

In addition to needing quiet, I've almost completely lost the ability to multitask. Mind you, this doesn't stop me from trying. Whenever the Internet connection slows down, my husband asks me how many tabs I have open. I say "not many" and then close three or four.

I'm slowly weaning myself off multitasking. I find I get a lot more done (a lot better) when I concentrate on just one thing at a time. I'm beginning to suspect that multitasking is more an avoidance mechanism than an efficiency tool. Better to do one thing well than two or three things in a slapdash manner. I suggest depressives try to stay away from dealing with too many things all at once.

Forgetfulness

Forgetfulness gets pricey. First of all, there are late fees and penalties for missed appointment or payment due dates. At $30 to $50 a pop, these add up quickly. Missed sales can also cost you quite a bit. Paying retail always stings, but paying retail knowing that yesterday this item was half the cost? That just *hurts*.

Your strongest ally in the war against forgetfulness is a calendar, be it a digital or physical one. When I refer to our wall calendar as "my memory," people think I'm joking. But I can never remember where we're supposed to be unless I check it. I forget that I even *have* appointments, let alone the dates and times, until I see it scribbled on there.

If there's a sale I can't miss – especially if I have a special coupon, store cash or freebie – I even write that on the calendar. I put notes on the beginning and end dates of the offers, plus a reminder halfway through. This gives me a fighting chance of remembering to use it.

I also find it helpful to keep paper and pens all around the house. That way I can make notes for chores I've just remembered I need to do, phone calls I need to make, grocery lists and pretty much anything that I don't trust my brain to hold onto. (Which is just about everything.)

One of the biggest frustrations, though, is getting home from the grocery store and realizing I've forgotten something. I've gone into the store to buy two items and walked out without one of them – but with bags full of plenty of other things. (Frugal tips: Never shop while hungry and always stick to your list.)

So you may want to keep a dry erase board or set of Post-It Notes on the fridge. Each time you run out of something, write it down immediately. Make it a habit to check the list before you leave for the store. Better yet, put the list on your phone, and you'll always have it on hand.

But you don't have to wait until you run out. Keep a list of things you often run out of but never remember to buy. It takes me several trips to remember to buy toothpaste, contact lens solution, Q-tips and, for some reason, bread.

If you keep a list of those oft-forgotten items, you can check it before you leave for the store and also while shopping online. There's nothing like checking out, either in person or online, and realizing half an hour later that you forgot to re-up on antacids.

Indecision

Depression can make it hard to decide. I mean, sometimes. Maybe. Sorta.

But seriously: If this illness makes us think poorly of ourselves, how could it not affect our ability to make decisions? How can we trust ourselves to choose correctly?

Sometimes delaying a decision works to our advantage. When you finally decide to go for it, the item might have been marked down. If you leave a website with items in your cart, the company may send you a "Come back!" discount.

But indecision can also be our downfall. Waiting too long may mean we wind up buying at retail. (We might even have to pay for expedited shipping.) Or we hem and haw for so long that the item is sold out, and then we either have to do without or buy a more expensive version.

Just do it

To add insult to injury, indecision is *exhausting*. It sucks away valuable mental energy that could be used on other things. While it's understandable to want to save a few bucks, it's not worth it if you end up too worn out to deal with other areas of your life.

Don't get me wrong: Big purchases absolutely need time and careful thought. Don't take the plunge on the next car you see just because you're sick of thinking about an auto purchase. But in most cases your focus may be best spent elsewhere.

In the end, the best things to do are:

1. Automate: The more things that are automatic, the fewer decisions you have to make. Having discounts on auto-refills means you don't have to worry about scouting sales. It also means never paying a premium for a last-minute replacement.
2. Use a decision tree. (More on that below)
3. Accept the suboptimal option: *Sometimes you're not going to get the best price*. If you buy now and find it cheaper somewhere else, catalog the deal for the next time you need a similar product. Then move on.

Ask the right questions

A good decision tree, especially during times of indecision, ought to help ease the "should I/shouldn't I?" mental strife.

The tree is merely a set of questions designed to that help you arrive at the best choice without sapping too much time or mental energy. For example:

1) Do I need this right now?
   a) If so, then buy it.
   b) If not, then ask:
2) Have I put this off before?
   a) If not, consider walking away until you're calmer.
   b) If so, then ask:
3) Is this a significantly better price than retail?
   a) If not, is it safe to wait for a sale?

     (1) If so, then don't act now – but do mark your calendar so that you buy in time. Don't forget to factor in shipping times if you're buying online.

     (2) Otherwise, just buy it. Even if you're not saving money, you're saving yourself the stress of trying to do without until a sale comes along.

   b) If the savings *are* significant, am I likely to find a better sale? If so, then ask:

      (1) How much energy will I need to put into finding/taking advantage of the better sale?
      (2) Is that energy worth the savings?

Your questions may vary slightly, depending on the item in question or your own priorities. The point is that you can run through the questions relatively quickly and arrive at an answer. You'll feel good that you thought it through, and you won't spend hours going back and forth.

Of course, sometimes you have an even harder question: whether you should buy an item at all. That's a whole different decision tree:

1. Does this fill a need, or did I think one up to rationalize the purchase?
2. How big a hassle is the current need? Would the purchase prevent a minor inconvenience or make things significantly easier?
3. Will this *really* save me time/effort/money, or am I just rationalizing?
4. How much effort will I have to put into maintaining it? (A hand-wash only item, something with a filter that needs to be replaced, a Mogwai that can't get wet, etc.)
5. If it's a lot of effort, how likely is it that I'll reliably put in/be able to put in the effort? (Hand-washing an item regularly, replacing a filter on schedule, Scotchguarding Gizmo, etc.)
6. Even if I'm willing to do it, is the extra effort worth the savings or ease this product would create?

These questions should give you a realistic look at how the item would get used. Then you can decide whether or not it's worth buying.

Of course, the method isn't foolproof. Sometimes you'll be wrong. Sometimes you'll end up rationalizing something that actually costs you time, money and hassle. Sometimes you'll talk yourself out of buying something that would have been worth it.

But no one gets things right 100% of the time. Use each error in judgment as an object lesson for making future decisions.

And no matter what you're trying to decide on, set a definitive deadline. You shouldn't spend too much time and energy on relatively small decisions. Besides, if you're consumed with one decision, you run the risk of not noticing other savings opportunities.

Inertia

Depressives often spend our downtime time picking ourselves apart. It's easy to obsess over all the things not getting done when we go to bed early or try to sleep in, or even when we just lie down for an hour. We spend too much of our resting time... *not* resting.

Hence, inertia – not a tendency toward inertness, but rather an inability to move. The problem is that most people fight this feeling, which may be the wrong tactic.

Instead, lean into it. Your mind and/or body may be telling you that you need to rest. If you feel utterly unable to handle a single thing, if all you want to do is curl up on the couch and watch "Law & Order" reruns... Do that. But first give yourself permission.

Take a sick day from your life. Because you *are* sick. Other than Ferris Bueller, people use sick days to get better. They rest. They let themselves heal. People with food poisoning don't try to do housework in between trips to the bathroom. They spend their non-vomiting hours trying to recuperate.

Follow their lead (minus the emesis). Allow yourself to do nothing. If guilt creeps in, tell yourself firmly that you're ill. That now is the time for healing.

Likely you'll find that letting yourself rest – truly rest – makes you more capable the next day. And if time is tight, at least allow yourself an hour or two of quiet. By giving yourself space to feel sick, you may just give yourself the ability to feel better.

And if you don't feel ready to take on the world the next day? Well, that could be a problem. You can't avoid life forever. If the inertia malingers, then you have to take steps. Tiny, tiny steps.

Go back and read over my advice about breaking things down. But forget putting things in bite-sized pieces – try taking it down to the sub-atomic-particle level. Create steps that you can manage, however small they may feel.

Need to call to make an appointment? Check to see if you can make it online. HealthGrades will let you set an appointment with many doctors' offices online. If that's not an option, see if a company's website has an e-mail option. You can write to them to set up an appointment that way. Be sure to specify what days and times of day would work best, and ask them to email you back.

If you can't do it electronically, try this:

- Look up the number on your computer, then leave the window/tab open.
- An hour later, write it down.
- An hour later, put the phone by the number.
- An hour later, dial the number in (but don't hit "Talk").
- An hour later, hit "Redial" then "Talk" and make the appointment

If you need customer support from a company, e-mail your question. It will almost certainly take longer to get a response, so don't e-mail them about something that needs to be resolved the same day. Still, as long as you stay on top of things – remember the calendar? – you can probably avoid actual phone interaction.

Or suppose you need to clean a sink or shower. Start by keeping a stash of products that do most of the work for you like Kaboom or Scrubbing Bubbles. Unfortunately, they don't do the whole job for you, so:

- Get the cleaning agent out of the cupboard.
- An hour later, put it by the area that needs cleaning.

- An hour later, spray the area.
- Wait as long as you can (without the cleaning agent drying up) then wipe it down.
- Throw away the paper towels/rinse the cleaning rags.

Need to tidy up? First of all, do you *actually* need to or would your energy be better spent elsewhere? If you must clean, then:

- Decide on one area – keep it *very* small.
- One hour later, grab a timer/pull up a timer app on your phone.
- An hour later, set the timer for five minutes.
- An hour later, hit "start" and clean.
- When the timer goes off, stop.

Need to hit a sale? First, check to see if you can buy online. If so:

- Pull up the website.
- An hour later, put the item(s) in your cart.
- An hour later, check out.

If it's not online, take these steps (with at least 30 minutes between each one):

- Decide what store you want to go to. *Store*, singular.
- Write down the exact items you need.
- Decide on the time you want to go.
- Put your wallet and keys in plain view.
- Put on your jacket.
- Take your wallet, keys and list and leave the house.

If even small steps feel too difficult, it's time to call in reinforcements. Ask a partner, relative or friend to come over. Just having someone there, cheering you on (and maybe even helping) can be huge.

Asking for that support probably won't be easy. The low self-esteem accompanying depression can make it hard to believe that people want to help, let alone that we're worthy of it. But they do. And we are.

People want to help but they don't always know how. The folks who care about you might actually be relieved if you can ask for something tangible: a grocery run, a load of laundry, a favorite entrée.

Inertia happens because things seem overwhelming. We don't know how or where to start. So pick the simplest starting place you can and go. Bribe yourself if necessary. Do whatever it takes to get moving. Just getting started will help you build momentum. And if it doesn't? Knowing that you did *something* makes it easier to build on that achievement tomorrow.

Overspending

Some people spend money to make themselves feel better. They comfort themselves with food, clothes, gadgets or items for the house. Or they spend more because they're anxious about fitting in, which makes them more susceptible to marketing. Whatever the reason, some depressives feel a compulsion to spend more as they feel more and more ill at ease.

Once again, it's about *mindful* spending. If the cost isn't too bad and if you really find comfort in the items, the purchase might not be that big a deal. It's a problem only if the items don't help and/or cost too much.

Work on reminding yourself that this kind of spending causes more guilt than comfort. It might help to keep pictures of past mistakes in your wallet, near your credit or debit cards. Work with a friend or therapist to figure out what *will* make you feel better.

Manic swings

As noted, I'm bipolar II. The manic states make frugality a real challenge. Although the swings have evened out somewhat thanks to medication, I still get the occasional burst of speeding thoughts and restlessness and sometimes a touch of grandiosity.

As soon as I start recognizing the symptoms, I put myself on lockdown. Rather than go out, I try to use the extra energy to get more things done at house. Finally cleaning the shower is much better than hitting the stores and buying a bunch of new stuff.

However, I can't always stay home. I might have an appointment, something might need to be replaced, or Tim might just be desperate for a date night since I actually have some energy.

In those cases I just have to be careful. Each time I'm tempted to spend money I remind myself that I'm in a manic state. A good compromise has been having a meal at a sit-down (chain) restaurant, which feels like luxury but doesn't cost us a ton.

If I'm still restless, we use passes or discounted gift cards to see a movie, or I redeem a Groupon voucher for a facial. I keep frugal entertainment options on hand the same way I keep convenience food around the house. It's all about having easy, affordable solutions to recurrent problems.

Other suggestions for dealing with manic swings:

- Have a pre-set amount you're allowed to spend during such times. Take it out in cash and leave the debit/credit card home.

- Go out with a friend who'll keep you from unnecessary shopping, or at least from overbuying. If necessary, give him/her your credit and debit card to guard.
- Have a list of free or cheap activities that you can choose from when you're antsy.
- If the weather is good, bike/rollerblade/walk wherever you want to go. It'll help you burn off some of the restless energy.
- Work out. Seriously, mania is an amazing energy burst.

Finally, try to think through any purchase you make. Ask yourself if you'll really want this in a day, a week, a month. Sometimes you can't answer accurately, but a lot of the time you'll know that it's the most impulsive of impulse purchases. (Also, get in the habit of keeping the receipts. You can always take it back later.)

If you have a problem with online shopping during these swings, install a reminder through your logins. Making your username or password "ManicMe" or "PutThisBack" or "DoIReallyNeedThis?" might help derail you.

Anxiety

I put this one last because it's practically its own chapter. But anxiety is a very real symptom for many depressives, so it's important to cover thoroughly.

Unfortunately, anxiety takes too many forms for me to create an exhaustive list. However, I asked my blog readers for their experiences, and I'm using those as examples. Hopefully, they'll strike a chord with many of you – and perhaps the rest of you will be able to find a parallel for your own situation.

For reasons far too long to explain here, I went through a period of time – okay, several of them, if I'm being honest – where I had an overwhelming fear of zombie attack. The knowledge that the creatures aren't real was nothing compared to my gut-squeezing terror that the undead would break in at any second. (In my defense, our house has a lot of windows, and everyone knows zombies can bust right through those suckers!)

No matter how much I tried to tell myself that a fictional monster couldn't hurt me, the more frustrated I got. Rational thinking didn't work, and I felt stupid for my inability to overcome the fear.

But anxiety isn't logical. No matter what your panicked brain is telling you, you know that:

- The crowd *isn't* really closing in on you from all sides.
- Your bank account *isn't* spiraling out of control – especially not in the past hour.
- You *will not* find new, massive savings the 13th time through the sale ad.
- Statistically speaking, you're probably *not* going to be in a horrible car crash.
- Zombies *aren't* going to break in.

Unfortunately, facts don't help when you're in the midst of a fear-provoked adrenaline surge. Rational thoughts are hard to hear over the sounds of a racing heartbeat.

All of these fears have one common thread: *We feel powerless and/or vulnerable*. So to tame our anxieties, we need to find ways to feel safer and more in control – even if it's just symbolically.

My husband, bless him, never tried to rationalize away my fears. Instead he insisted that we keep his old samurai sword next to my side of the bed. He figured that I'd feel safer if I had a weapon.

The thing was old and probably horribly blunt. I doubt it'd have protected me against any real intruder, let alone one that isn't stopped by pain.

But that wasn't the point. The point is that I had a symbolic weapon against my fictitious enemy. (Also some screwdrivers around the house in case zombies struck when I was away from the sword. But the metaphor mostly stands.) I felt stronger and safer, which kept me calm enough to work on the deeper issues at play.

But not everyone has a samurai sword. You need to figure out your own way(s) to empower yourself and gain a sense of control.

Unfortunately, some of the ways we try to soothe ourselves can end up creating a feedback loop of mounting panic.

For example, checking a bank balance might not reassure you that your finances are just fine. In fact, it might just convince you that things are only under control *because* you keep checking your balances. Thus checking your balances proves only that you need to *keep* checking your balances.

The same could be said for people who get anxious driving. Each time you're not in an accident could prove that you're safe – or that you're one trip closer to disaster.

Checking sales flyers repeatedly and coming up with the same results probably means you've found all the savings. But some people would argue that they're just familiarizing themselves so that *next time* something new will jump out at them.

Even when coping mechanisms don't actually feed the anxiety, they take up large amounts of your time. It's no way to live. No matter how acceptable the show *Monk* made it look.

Checking your balance

One of my readers had times when she was convinced her finances were in freefall. She would counter that by checking her bank balance to reassure herself that nothing had changed. Unfortunately, any reprieve she felt was temporary. Inevitably the anxiety would return and she'd end up compulsively checking and re-checking her account. The compulsion only exacerbated her feelings of powerlessness.

So she created rules about how often she is allowed to check her balance. Now she can verify that the funds are still in there, but not obsess. In between these account reviews she forces herself to deal with the fear and uncertainty, or at least to distract herself from them.

Sometimes it's just about interrupting a negative train of thought. The reader reinforces her self-imposed rules with certain penalties. For example, if she checks the account too often she has to donate $20 of her fun money to a charity.

This is perfect because it's a *positive* penalty. She feels the sting of losing the funds but at least it's going to a good cause. It's enough to encourage her to self-soothe without making her feel too bad about giving away the money.

If you take this route, be sure to set reasonable goals. If you're currently checking your account every half hour, a goal of twice a week isn't going to work. Start with every 45 minutes, then move it up to every hour. Give yourself a short period of adjustment, then challenge yourself with a longer lengths of time.

While you're setting these rules, set up as many bank account alerts as possible. You might worry less about checking if you're notified every time your balance dips below $50, $100, $150 – or whatever number would help you feel safe.

Budgeting software may also help with this, since it will send you e-mails as you reach your spending limits. This lets you remain vigilant without succumbing to the need for near-constant bank logins.

Driving/being in public

One reader said that driving is a huge source of anxiety. She only goes to stores that are close to her home even if it means missing out on sales. I imagine people who have trouble being out in public or in crowds have similar issues.

Honestly I don't consider this a financial deal-breaker. I've already made my feelings clear about the benefits of even suboptimal stock-ups. If being out and about is going to drain you that much – which means less coping ability for other areas of life – maybe you should just skip the sales. There are worse things in the world.

But maybe you can't accept (or afford) the extra expense. In that case, the first thing to consider is even more automation.

Ordering online means you have to go out less. Great deals on a lot of products are available on the Web, especially when you use cash back sites. Our old friend auto-delivery is a big help, and some grocery stores will deliver for a small fee. (The fee may be more than covered by the extra savings.) This lets you shop for the best prices without the anxiety of driving longer distances.

Or try the buddy system. Take a friend or partner with you. Having company might relax you, and if you do have a panic attack in public you'll have someone to shoo other people out of your personal space and, if necessary, drive you home.

Speaking of which: If you're afraid of driving, maybe being a passenger would help. It might be easier going places if you're not the one maneuvering thousands of pounds of machinery around other people. (It could also be worse, since you have less control. Trial and error, I'm afraid.)

Ads/coupons

Another reader told me that she becomes obsessed with poring over grocery and other sale ads. She just can't stop, convinced that she can still save a few more cents. I'm afraid frugality has its own version of FOMO.

I'm guessing plenty of people have similar issues. They check ads over and over, terrified that they're missing something, that some savings are eluding their grasp.

I have four words for that group: *Yes, you absolutely are*.

Before you start freaking out, consider these facts:

- There's usually at least one store that doesn't have a location near you: Aldi's, BJ's Warehouse, etc.
- Even if you do have every chain at your disposal, it's virtually impossible to hit every one.
- Even if you coupon avidly, there will probably always be a couple that you forget to clip or that got lost in the shuffle.
- You're probably not part of a coupon swap group, so you can't get extra ones for maximum savings on stock-ups.

Look, there are billions of people in the world. Surely one of them is smarter – or at least more diligent – than you. So yes, you will always miss out on *some* savings. Try to relax a little and give yourself permission to be imperfect.

But since logic often fails to penetrate anxiety, here's something else to consider: Are the extra savings really worth it? Spending 20 minutes to find $20 of savings is great. Spending another 15 minutes for $5 of savings… Well, that's worth it to some people. But after a certain point, the savings you find will necessarily become smaller and smaller.

It's an issue of diminishing returns. You're putting more and more effort in for smaller and smaller savings. After two hours of study, you might find an extra $10 to save. And you might save a couple of bucks by going to an entirely different store for a single item. But how much are your time, energy and sanity worth?

Once again, structure comes to the rescue.

Setting up auto-refills will cut down on the number of deals you need to find. We have toilet paper, shaving gel, cat food and even peanut butter delivered, preferring to get a pretty good price all the time than to constantly look for sales and coupons.

Create limits for yourself – for example, the amount of time you spend reviewing the ads, the number of times you look them over or the amount of new savings you find each time. Or it could be a combination. For example, you might decide to stop when:

- You've looked at the ads five times, or
- Spent more than hour on it, or
- Your latest review yielded less than $3 in new savings.

You could also just rely on the experts. As I mentioned earlier in the book, sites like Coupon Mom match sales and coupons for stores across the country. The lists are exhaustive – they're compiled by people who review ads and coupons as their full-time job – so you don't have to worry about missing something.

Then you just have to decide which savings are worth your time and energy. You may find that you're content with savings at a small number of stores, just as my reader found it easier to check her bank balance less often.

But it's something you probably need to winnow down over time. Eventually, you'll find a level where you feel less anxious without spending all of your time and energy on shopping.

Price comparisons

Several readers say they're anxious about being frugal "enough." The worry was particularly strong when it comes to comparing prices. They get anxious if they feel there isn't enough time to research prices.

Making purchases on a deadline is nerve-wracking. Panic sets in, which makes it harder to think, which convinces you that you're going to make a suboptimal decision, which exacerbates the panic.

The first thing to do is to figure out whether there actually *is* a deadline. At times I find that I've somehow manufactured panic. It's probably because I dread decision-making. I want it to be over quickly, so I find myself believing that the purchase has to be made immediately.

When I realize the deadline isn't real, I try to walk away from the decision. This reminds me that that I have plenty of time. It lets me come back when I'm in a calmer, more rational frame of mind.

Of course, sometimes the deadline *is* real. In that case, you need limits for your search and decision times. The Internet has a near-endless supply of four things: information, opinions, trolls and deals.

Even when you have plenty of time you can't ever be sure you've found the best price. So why expect yourself to perform an exhaustive search when time is of the essence? Instead, it's another case of triage.

Have a certain number of websites and stores that you're allowed to check. In a calmer moment, you may want to create a list of the best stores and sites for specific categories like household, personal care and electronics. That way you don't have to worry about forgetting an obvious one in a fog of panic.

If you need the item immediately, I'd suggest checking no more than two stores or three websites. Yes, you might end up overpaying a bit but at least you'll have it. Besides, it's impossible to be sure you got the best price, unless only one store is selling the item. Even then, you can't know whether a sale (or a better item) will come along.

But what about when you have plenty of time?

Because of the wealth of choices, you'll need to create a logical stopping point. This could be the number of websites you check, the time you spend searching or the difference in savings. For example, you may decide to stop when you've:

- Checked more than six sites, or
- Spent more than an hour looking, or
- Found that the difference between the two lowest prices is less than $3

You could also choose to let someone else do the heavy lifting. Sites like Bizrate and PriceGrabber will scour the Internet for you; just type in the item you need and you'll get a list of stores offering the lowest prices.

Just as with your own efforts, the searches won't be exhaustive. But these sites can be a godsend if you're in a real hurry or just want the professionals to do it for you.

Running the numbers

One reader told me that she sometimes can't stop running the budget numbers. She and her husband have enough, but sometimes that doesn't feel true to her. She doesn't trust the positive numbers she comes up with. They don't make her feel secure.

If you're experiencing something similar, the first step is probably to use Excel to create your budget. You might believe the numbers more if you're using a program that does the math for you.

The next step is counterintuitive: increase the budget limits. This isn't a license to spend more – in fact, the increase might only exist in an Excel sheet – but it could help reassure you. If your spending goes up and you still have a positive balance, you'll know you have enough.

No matter what, you need to limit how often you're allowed to run the numbers. Set a maximum number of times per month, and make a rule about how far apart the checks can happen. Or decide that you have to stop checking once the numbers come out the same three times (or four or five) in a row.

Then focus on something positive about that positive bank balance. For example, you might think about it going to an emergency fund, general savings, retirement contributions, a future vacation or some other goal.

Or perhaps you need to distract yourself from money entirely. Play with your pet, call a friend, watch a movie, take up needlepoint. (Think how helpful it'll be to see "The budget is done; look at this pretty pillow" on your couch.)

That's all, folks

Well, there you have it: my alleged wisdom on the subject of saving money amid depression.

I've spent the last eight years wading through the excrement of expectations – both society's and my own. I slowly and painfully learned to listen to my physical and emotional limitations. Then I even more slowly and more painfully learned to accept them.

It's my hope that these tips and insights will help you find much shorter and less draining routes to a balance between frugality and depression.

Don't forget to concentrate on just one hack at a time. Two, tops. Anything more and you're begging for it all to come crashing down. Take it from someone who knows.

And finally, if you take one lesson away from this book (other than how many stores are on cash back sites), it should be this: Be kind to yourself. Forgiving yourself your limitations is the best and smartest way to navigate all aspects of life. It's especially important when working toward any type of change. Even if that's just the change of saving your change.

Afterword

This book started as a post called, you guessed it, "Frugality for Depressives." Unfortunately, it refused to stay post-sized. I tried splitting it into two, but nothing quite worked.

I came to the unfortunate conclusion that I was going to have to write a short book. Emphasis on "short" since I had several other things that needed my time and attention. So I sucked it up and figured I'd write a 10ish page book. Twenty, tops.

I'm typing this afterword on the 98th page of in a Word document. Apparently I had a bit more to say than expected.

There's probably plenty of other things I could have added; but honestly, I'm exhausted and stressed. I have no idea why people write books voluntarily.

And that's the thing: I don't feel like this book was voluntary. Once the idea sprang to mind, it wouldn't rest. It nagged at me. It made me feel guilty (not that this is hard to do). It sat on the edge of my brain like an insolent toddler, sticking its tongue out and otherwise making me pay attention.

I wrote this not out of hopes for huge profits – I know what most writers make from self-publishing – but because there's nothing out there like it. Because, Big Pharma commercials aside, depression is still too taboo to consider depressives as an audience for anything other than self-help books.

But sad people are people too, eh? I've spent several years blogging about Tim's and my travails – the good and the bad – and about what I joke is our deeply imperfect form of frugality.

And while I haven't had groundbreaking success, I *have* found a dedicated set of readers – ones who like conversations about living with depression, chronic illness and other things that breed a very jaded and insightful (if slightly brittle) sense of humor. They appreciate my honesty, and I appreciate the chance to have my ego stroked for my navel gazing. It's a very symbiotic relationship.

Seriously though, my readers are my friends and my support system. They've been there for some truly awful times in my life. They've discussed difficult things that go on in theirs. Sometimes the subject of money even comes up!

I know these people, and I feel protective of them. So it drives me crazy (ha ha) that people like me, like them, are still considered a negligible demographic. Has no one seen recent statistics? Approximately one in every 10 Americans is depressed. Worldwide, around 350 million people suffer from the condition.

This isn't some rare condition. It's just one that no one is talking about. And so just in case we depressives didn't have enough to contend with, the burden falls on us to keep the conversation going. It's up to us to be honest about our struggles so that others struggling know that they're not abnormal. (Well, other than their brain chemistry.)

I know a how-to book – let alone one on money management – may not be the perfect way to start the conversation. But at least it's something. I leave it to the rest of you to keep the discussion going.

One last thing: If you haven't read *Shoot the Damn Dog* by Sally Brampton, do so now. It's a breathtakingly painful, eloquent account of depression. My copy is hopelessly marked up. It's perhaps the best book written about depression – other than this one, obviously.

www.ingramcontent.com/pod-product-compliance
Lightning Source LLC
Chambersburg PA
CBHW070247190526
45169CB00001B/332